Soccer iQ Presents...
High Pressure

How to Win Soccer Games by Smothering Your Opponent

BY DAN BLANK

ISBN: 0989697770
ISBN 13: 9780989697774

For Izzy

If you'd like to purchase copies of this book for everyone on your team at a discounted rate, just contact me through the soccerpoet.com website.

I hope you'll be my Twitter friend. My handle is @SoccerPoet.

TABLE OF CONTENTS

INTRODUCTION

I was at a recruiting event somewhere on the east coast. It was the mid-1990s, so I don't recall exactly when or where. I couldn't guess at how many of these events I've been to, and I've forgotten more than I remember. But I remember this one – or at least a moment from this one. This was the one where a sixteen-year-old girl I'd never met changed my life. Okay, maybe that's an exaggeration. Maybe she didn't exactly *change my life*, but she certainly impacted it. This is the one where a sixteen-year-old stranger gave me absolute clarity.

These days, when it comes to recruiting events, coaches must magically appear at five different fields in every single time slot. Back then, the demands on my time weren't so pressing. In other words, my schedule had gaps. To fill the gaps I would look for any club I enjoyed watching, and then go sit down at their game, even if I wasn't recruiting a player from that field.

One of those gaps was upon me, and while trying to figure out precisely how to kill an hour and a half of free time, I spotted the dazzling green jerseys that were a singular indicator of a club from St. Louis called J.B. Marine. Marine played a beautiful brand of soccer and had been churning out quality players for years. Ninety minutes with J.B. Marine was time well spent, so I wandered over to their match.

I got to the sideline a minute before kickoff as the players took their spots on the field. Then there was that typical, quiet calm as everyone waited for the referee's whistle to get things underway. And then one of Marine's players – a center back I think – shattered the silence. In a voice that boomed like a clap of thunder, she shouted, "Make 'em hate it, Marine!" The way she said it – well, it was pretty darn convincing. It wasn't like she was dabbling in this match. This girl wasn't dipping her toes in the water. She was wholly committed to the mission. She genuinely wanted to make the opponent hate it. And me, well, I was hooked!

Make 'em hate it! It gave me chills. It was my new favorite sound. And it's a saying I would put in my pocket and go on to use hundreds of times with my own teams.

Make 'em hate it! Could you say much more with four words? It's a declaration of war. It's a commitment to this competitive ideal that we're going to make your life so miserable for the next ninety minutes that you'll actually be happy when the game is over.

I love that.

Make 'em hate it! I can't think of a saying that is more emblematic of a well-executed style of high-pressure soccer. In possession soccer, we make the opponent hate it when we have the ball. With high pressure, we make them hate it when *they* have the ball. And when it works, it's a thing of beauty.

In high pressure, you press the opponent to the point of suffocation. You tighten the vice and widespread panic ensues. You see it in the body language of the opposing players, particularly the defenders, who suddenly want nothing to do with the ball. When the ball finds them, their every movement screams, "Get that thing away from me!" They're rattled. Composure deserts them and technique quickly follows. They stop plotting their next pass because they aren't thinking about winning; they're just clinging to survival. Instead of moving into seams to find the ball, they start hiding behind opponents. Each one of them is preoccupied with the idea of not being the player who gave away the ball that ended up in the goal. And when you see opposing players acting like that, you know you're making them hate it.

High-pressure is the purest form of soccer. I'm not saying that makes it the best. I'm just saying that if you took two teams of kids who had never really been tactically trained and stuck them on the field with a ball and told them to go play a game, those teams would play high-pressure soccer without even knowing what it was called. When the opponent has the ball, regardless of where on the field that happens to be, you go and try to take it from them because you need the ball to win. Where the ball goes, you go. It just seems to make sense. Show me any game of U-10 soccer and I'll show you two teams playing high pressure. High pressure is a soccer player's default setting.

With that in mind, there doesn't seem to be much savvy to high-pressure soccer: See the ball, chase the ball, take the ball. It would seem that it's all just a matter of athleticism, determination and work rate. It's so easy a nine-year-old could do it. However...

High pressure is in fact much more nuanced than simply applying blunt force trauma. I'll concede that it might not require as much tactical savvy as a low-pressure, counter-attacking style, but it's far more complex than just run, chase, hit. Just because nine-year-olds do it, that doesn't mean they do it well.

Like any other style of soccer, high pressure will give you varying degrees of effectiveness depending on how well your pressure is organized. The goal of this book is to help you organize your pressure in the most efficient and effective way possible so that you may inflict maximum physical and emotional damage to your opponent. Additionally, we will be discussing the strengths and weaknesses of both high- and low-pressure systems as well as the variables to consider when choosing your system of pressure. Finally, I will do my best to convey the points of emphasis that will help you convince your players to buy into your system because, after all, if your players don't buy in, your system doesn't really matter.

Let's dispense with a couple of housekeeping matters before we begin. I often interchange the terms *style* and *system*. Some coaches might not like that. Hopefully they'll forgive me. Traditionally, a system is how you set up your formation, such as a 4-4-2. High pressure is a style of team defense. I get it. But since we're talking about a systematic approach to pressure, I didn't think it would cause too much confusion if I referred to high pressure as a system.

Additionally, I bounce back and forth between gender references, as opposed to using strictly male or strictly female pronouns throughout the text. Although I attempted to limit each particular topic to one gender at a time, it is possible, nay, highly likely, that somewhere in these pages you will be reading about a left wing who is a he in one paragraph only to magically become a she in the next paragraph. I apologize for any confusion you must endure.

Likewise, you will note that while I mostly write to coaches, occasionally I appear to be writing to (or talking to) players. I can't help it. I spent two decades talking to players. I like talking to players. That's what coaches do. I hope you'll humor me.

Some of the full-field diagrams don't include all 22 players but only the ones relevant to illustrating whatever point I'm trying to make. If players are missing, it's just to make the diagram easier to understand.

You will encounter many generalizations throughout this text. When I offer a description, I am working from a picture in my head. I'll do my best to describe that picture, but as this is a book and not video, it is likely that from time to time, the picture in your head won't perfectly align with the picture in my head. I tend to think in broad strokes – commonalities if you will. I'll offer scenarios that I've encountered with the greatest frequency. There are many exceptions to these scenarios. And if you're a coach, those exceptions will come rushing to the forefront and you'll want to shout, *"But what about when this happens!"* It's impossible for a book to cover every scenario that will surface in a soccer match, so in those moments, let's just agree that you're right.

There is a multitude of coaching philosophies about pressing. This book presents one way – my way. Please don't let it dissuade you from learning others. There are parts of this book you will agree with, and parts you may not. I encourage you to incorporate the parts that you find useful into your own team and to leave the rest behind.

Thank you for reading this book. I hope you enjoy it and that it helps your team. Most of all, I hope it helps you create the kind of team that I wouldn't want to play against. I'm giving you what I can. The rest is up to you.

Make 'em hate it.

PRESSING

1

What is High Pressure?

To understand what high pressure is, we should probably start with what it's not. In spite of its title, high pressure is not an anxiety-laced, do-or-die, run-around-like-your-hair's-on-fire state of being. It's not an attitude. Well, at least, it's not *just* an attitude. Pressure is your team's concerted effort to dispossess the opponent. High is merely where you'll make that effort. High means closer to the opponent's goal; low means closer to the goal you're defending. High pressure is simply a tactical decision that your team will press the opponent high up the field and try to force turnovers in your attacking third or attacking half.

High pressure is a tactical choice you get to make. So is low pressure – a style in which you invite the opponent closer to your own goal before embarking on your mission to win back the ball.

There are a lot of people who hear 'high pressure' and think *urgency* or *intensity* or *desperation*. But that's a little misleading. I mean, regardless of where you decide to set up your defense, you want your players defending with urgency and intensity, yes? A simple comparison can be drawn from basketball where a full-court press would be considered high pressure and a half-court defense considered low pressure. Just because a basketball team elects to defend in a half-court set, that doesn't mean the players defend lackadaisically. They still have to work their tails off; they're just doing that work in a different part of the court.

When we set our team up in a high-pressure style, our objective is to press the opponents close to their own goal whenever prudent and to force turnovers, preferably in our attacking third of the field. That is the governing idea behind a high-pressure style of team defense.

Now theoretically, high pressure is a style of team defending. It's about ball-recovery *after* an attack has fizzled; it's what you do after you've *unintentionally* lost the ball. However, there are teams that use high pressure as the launch pad for their attack. In other words, these teams aren't necessarily looking to build an attack by passing their way up the field. Instead they set out to make soccer a game of territory, and some of them do it quite well. Their plan is to get the ball in behind the opposing defense, usually by angling balls towards the corners of the eighteen, and to then press the defenders as they retrieve the ball while facing their own end-line. By putting opposing defenders in difficult situations, these teams hope to cause turnovers in dangerous areas of the field and to turn those turnovers into scoring chances.

In spite of that last paragraph, please understand that utilizing a high pressure defense doesn't have to dictate or dilute your attacking style. You can employ high pressure defense and still play beautiful soccer. Barcelona, a fantastic pressing team, has also been the world's best at possessing the ball. They are quite unlike any team described in the previous paragraph. They don't dump and chase. They don't donate possession to the opponent. They don't use pressure as the start of their attack; they use pressure to regain the ball once possession has been lost.

My point is that high pressure is not an all-or-none proposition. *High-pressure* and *possession soccer* are not mutually exclusive terms. You can, in fact, have both. I'll give you the keys to effectively press; it's up to you to decide how to employ them.

2

High Pressure or Pressing?

There's a difference between high pressure and pressing. The terms are often used interchangeably, but there is a difference.

Pressing is the act of putting pressure on the ball and it can happen anywhere on the field. High-pressure is a systematic, big-picture effort to dispossess the opponent in its defensive third or defensive half of the field. Pressing is a moment; high-pressure is a design.

Even a low-pressure team will periodically press up high during the course of a game. For example, let's say a low-pressure team wins the ball in its own defensive third and launches a counterattack that moves the ball deep into enemy territory. It's got the opponent on the ropes as the ball is pinging around the eighteen-yard box. Then the ball skips in to the opposing center back who happens to be at the penalty spot facing his own goal. Assuming that there are some attacking players nearby, it doesn't make sense to turn tail and retreat back to your restraining line just because the other team has the ball, right? In this scenario it makes much more sense for the low-pressure team to press up high because the risk-reward ratio is very favorable. They are still in a good position to recover the ball in a dangerous area and create a goal-scoring opportunity. So they press up high.

By that same token, a high-pressure team will periodically find its forwards defending close to or even inside its own eighteen. There's no point in standing thirty yards from the opponent's goal when the ball is deep in your end of the field. My point is this: It doesn't matter if you are a high-pressure team or a low-pressure team or something in between, the game will often dictate where you are pressing the ball. Regardless of where you set a restraining line, or even if you play with no restraining line at all, players have to move in accordance with the ball.

3

Why High Pressure? (Part 1)

The obvious reason to choose high pressure is that when you're successful, your team is winning the ball close to the opponent's goal and obviously that can lead to more immediate scoring chances. If you win the ball up high, you have a shorter field to cover and likely fewer opponents between you and the goal. In short, you have an easier path to the goal. Additionally, in a high-pressure scheme, you're making it as difficult as possible for the opponent to move the ball into your end of the field. In a lower-pressure set-up, your team will concede part of the field to the opponent. In a pure high-pressure set, you concede nothing and the opponent must earn every inch of territory.

With that kind of logic you may be asking yourself why a team would choose to play any other way. Well, there are some excellent reasons and we'll discuss them in the next chapter.

4

The Case against High Pressure

The objective of high pressure – winning the ball close to the opponent's goal – makes any other style seem intrinsically weak, illogical, dull and counterproductive. And yet, at soccer's highest levels, we regularly see teams defend with a low-pressure style. Why is that?

Frederick the Great once said, "He who defends everything defends nothing." That's the long and short of the case against high pressure defending: You're defending everything.

Here's how a coaching course instructor explained team defending to me: When the opponent has the ball, your ten field-players form your defensive block. Think of that block as a blanket that's too short for your bed. If you use that blanket to cover your head, your feet are left exposed. If the blanket covers your feet, your head is exposed. And if the blanket covers both your head and your feet, it's because you've ripped a giant hole through the middle.

When the opponent has the ball, it has roughly 9,000 square yards of field to work with. In a high-pressure system, eleven players are responsible for defending that entire parcel of land. That's a lot of ground to cover. The idea is to move our blanket in relation to the ball. If the ball is near the opponent's goal, we pull the blanket up to cover our head, leaving our feet exposed. When the ball moves into our end of the field, we immediately pull the blanket down toward our feet. As the soccer ball can move very quickly from one end of the field to the other and back again, we run the very real risk of stretching out our blanket. When our blanket starts getting stretched, we rip holes in the middle. When or blanket has holes in the middle, our team is very vulnerable.

A low-pressure style shrinks the field. If you play an all-out high-pressure style, your team has to defend end-line to end-line along 120 yards of field. But in a low-pressure set, where you set a restraining line at the top of the center circle (for example), you are conceding the first fifty yards. Now you are defending a seventy-yard field. You're using your blanket to cover your feet and not your head.

Additionally, a low-pressure system keeps your ten field players more tightly grouped because the offside law becomes more of a factor. Let's say you're in a high-pressure set and your forwards are pressing the opponent along the end-line. Your lowest defenders are going to be right near midfield – they can't go much further because the offside law offers no protection in the opponent's half of the field – so you have ten field-players stretched out over sixty yards. In a low-pressure style, the line of defenders tends to be much closer to the line of forwards. If the forwards are confronting the ball at the top of the center circle, the lowest defenders will probably be no more than ten yards behind the bottom of the center circle. Now the distance from your lowest player to your highest player is roughly thirty yards. And, because your defenders are in your half of the field, they are setting the offside line. This makes for a much more congested space that the opponent must navigate with the ball.

Think of it this way: If I told you to run the length of a bowling lane without touching any of the pins, you'd be fine until you actually reached the pins.

Because they are so tightly packed at the far end of the lane, you would struggle to complete the task. But if we spread those ten pins over the length of the entire lane, you could navigate them with ease. That's the difference between a field that is congested and one that isn't. A low-pressure system allows you to incorporate the offside law to keep your pins more tightly packed. That's one of the benefits of a low-pressure defense.

It's also important to understand that high pressure is a double-edged sword. When your forwards are pressuring the opposing defenders near their own eighteen, your defenders will be pressed up into the opponent's half of the field. The most dangerous space is the area behind your defenders and in front of your goalkeeper. As your defenders move up the field, that space gets bigger, and that leaves you vulnerable. In other words, high pressure leaves you susceptible to balls played in behind your defense. When all of your field players are pushed up into the attacking half of the field, you are most susceptible to counterattacks.

Let me give you a very common, practical example. How many times have you seen a one-goal lead turn into a two-goal win in the final five minutes of a match? It happens all the time because the trailing team needs to chase the game to find an equalizer. So they frantically send more bodies forward and throw everything they've got into winning the loose ball that's bouncing around in the opponent's eighteen. Next thing you know, the opponent breaks pressure and is off to the races. A midfielder emerges from the pack and slips a ball in behind the defense and the story ends with the insurance goal. That's the danger of a high-pressure set and committing numbers forward.

A few years back I was coaching a U-16 girls club team. We were a decent team, but we certainly weren't great and we definitely had some weak spots. All in all, we were just okay. But up top we had some legitimate weapons. Heck, we had an arsenal.

In U-16 girls soccer, almost every team plays a high pressure style; not necessarily by some grand coaching design, but just because the players will chase the ball wherever it goes and no one coaches them into playing any other way. Anyway, because we weren't a great team, we spent a lot of time in our own end. It wasn't too difficult for opponents to move the ball into our half of the field and keep it there for long stretches. My point is that we spent most of our time defending.

Despite all this, that team ended up winning the league title and going undefeated to boot. We won every stinkin' game. Yes, we had weaknesses, but the one thing we had in abundance was breakaway speed up top. We had three forwards who could absolutely fly! These girls weren't just fast for sixteen-year-olds; they were fast for college players. They all had top-tier, Division I speed. Typically, the three fastest players on the field were my left wing, my right wing and my center forward. And against teams that high-pressed us, that speed had a lot of field to work with.

Here's a scenario that occurred several times each game: The opponent would have the ball in our end for a sustained period of time and my players would be spinning like tops trying to defend. Then an errant pass would find its way to one of my players who would hoof the ball as far up the field as she could. The ball would clear the opposing line of defenders and then it was Breakaway City! We had more clear-cut 1v1s with the goalkeeper than any team I've ever seen. On my honor, we had three or four of those breakaways every game. And, also on my honor, there were times when all three of my forwards got in behind the opponent's entire defense. That's right – *three* players running at the goalkeeper. How many times have you seen that happen? As you would expect, when you get chances like that, you're going to score some goals, and that's how we won our league.

When the opponent had the ball deep in our end of the field, that's when we were the most dangerous. As counter-intuitive as that may seem, it was unmistakably true. We didn't have to build an attack. We didn't have to worry about stringing passes together and weaving our way down the field. We just needed one ball to clear the defense and those three forwards were long gone. Such is the inherent danger of having all of your players pushed into the attacking half of the field. When you play a high-pressure style, that is the fine line you walk because one big ball can beat your entire defense.

So back to our original question — Why would a team choose to set-up in something other than high-pressure?

When you choose a low-pressure style, you institute a restraining line (a topic we'll discuss in detail later) that moves your attackers back toward the goal you are defending. This, in turn, pushes your back line closer to your own goal, which shrinks the dangerous space between the defenders and the goal-keeper. This, in theory, keeps your defensive block compact and forces the opponent to pick its way through your ten field players as opposed to beating them all with one killer ball. Simply put, low pressure allows you to get a lot of bodies behind the ball and forces the opponent to play in a crowded space.

A high-pressure system also demands a high defensive work rate, particularly from your forwards, because they are going to spend a good bit of their time and energy chasing and pressuring the opponent's defenders. At the professional level, where a team may be limited to three substitutions in a match, coaches don't want their goal-scorers burning through their fuel chasing opponents. They often prefer their forwards to spend their energy attacking instead of defending.

Some coaches will choose a low-pressure set-up when there is a mismatch in ability. If your team is outmatched in talent, you may decide that you're better off playing a low-pressure style that forces the opponent to pick its way through a crowded field. With that in mind, some teams choose to play a low-pressure style where they concede the first fifty or sixty yards of the field to the opponent and then attempt to counterattack upon a change of possession. Leicester City beautifully executed a low-pressure, counterattacking style to win the English Premier League in 2016. The club was 18th out of twenty teams in possession – and dead last in pass-success rate – but they managed to outmaneuver much wealthier clubs like Chelsea, Liverpool, Arsenal and Manchester City for the league title. With well-organized and often heroic defending, Leicester City distinguished itself as a team that could absorb long bouts of pressure close to its goal and then efficiently spring dangerous counterattacks.

And there we have one of the fundamental differences between the two styles: A high-pressure style is designed to create many chances of all varieties. A low-pressure style will likely generate fewer chances, but those chances can be exceptionally dangerous. As the coach, it's up to you to evaluate your personnel, evaluate your opponent, evaluate the conditions and then pick your poison.

I believe every team, from the age of fourteen and up, should be able to play in at least two different defensive schemes – a high-pressure set-up and then something with a lower restraining line – and to move fluidly between the two schemes during the course of a match. Why? Because sometimes the game dictates a change in your needs. For example, if you want your forwards to get a little breather late in the first half, you might move to a lower restraining line to ease their workload. If you're up 1-0 in the final ten minutes of a match, it might be wise to move out of high pressure and focus your energies on closing out the game. By that same token, if you're down by a goal late in the game, you'd better be able to high press. And the best reason of all to be able to shift from one style to the other is that the style you're using isn't working and you realize you'd be better off changing your restraining line. At that point you don't want to be thinking, *'Gosh, I wish we had gone over that at training.'* Moving from one style to the next isn't really something you can coach on the fly.

5

When High Pressure?

L et's say that you've gone out and taught your team to play in two different defensive schemes; one is all-out high pressure, and the other is with a restraining line across the top of the center circle. Now you've got some flexibility in your tactical set-up. At this point, maybe *Why High Pressure?* isn't the right question. Maybe the better question is: *When?* If your team is equally comfortable in either scheme, then it's up to you to figure out the right time to deploy one or the other. I can't give you these tips as gospel – there will always be exceptions – but generally speaking, here are some situations when you might wish to favor one or the other.

High Pressure

- I would recommend high pressure whenever you can get away with it. In other words, if you can consistently create turnovers high up the field and make it exceptionally difficult for the opponent to get out of its own end, then there's no point in inviting them closer to your goal. This is often a matter of the opponent's technical ability. If the opposing players aren't technically competent enough to break your pressure, then go after them. If you can consistently turn over the opponent close to its own goal, then I say go for it.

- Poor field conditions can be an invitation to high press, particularly if the opponent fancies itself as a possession team. Passing your way out of trouble gets infinitely more difficult on a field that is bumpy or wet.

- If the opponent doesn't have a speed threat up top, you might be more inclined to gamble and press up high, especially if you have some very fast defenders. If you are confident that their forwards can't outrun your backs, that gives you some freedom to press. This is a major consideration because you may decide that as a part of your press, your defenders are to deny any passes into the feet of the forwards. If that's how you want to play it, then you are daring the opponent to play over the top of you. If you don't think the opponent will take the bait, or if they won't win the foot races anyway, then that's a pretty strong motivator to press high up the park.

- If the opponent has a throw-in deep in its own territory, that can be an invitation to high press, even if you're playing from a lower-pressure set. Few players can get enough distance on a throw-in to cleanly break pressure and, even at the collegiate level, throw-ins are basically a coin flip when it comes to which team ends up with possession. Bottom line – it's hard to keep the ball and break pressure when restarting with a throw-in.

- If the opposing goalkeeper is bad with his/her feet, that might influence you to press high and chase back-passes to the 'keeper. I wouldn't use this as the sole justification for high-pressure, but it's worth factoring into your decision. By that same token, a goalkeeper who is phenomenal with her feet might make you rethink chasing those back-passes.

- If you need a goal, particularly late in a match, you've got no choice; you have to chase the game. When you have to make something happen, high pressure is the only option.

- In spite of all the reasons we've discussed not to press up high, sometimes you may want to press an opponent who outmatches you in talent. Don't get me wrong; I wouldn't necessarily suggest high pressing an opponent that absolutely dwarfs you in talent, but if the talent gap is close to manageable, it may be worth your while to go after the sacred cow. At the collegiate level, the best teams often face opponents who collapse into a low-pressure style specifically for that one game. They get used to seeing opponents who bunker and give them a ton of respect on the ball, and that can dull their edge. High pressing a team like that can be a big gamble – after all, there's a reason all those other teams have backed off. But, if you can get after them right out of the gates, you might be able to land a big, fat sucker punch that changes the entire psychological dynamic.

Low Pressure

- The most common reason that American players ever even learn a low-pressure system is because their team is about to face a much more talented opponent. The coach wants to make that opponent play through a very crowded field, especially near his own goal, so he sets a very low restraining line and puts a lot of numbers behind the ball. Knowing the opponent will have the lion's share of the ball, the coach's top priority is to keep the opponent from scoring with hopes that maybe his own team will pull a rabbit out of a hat and score on a counterattack and win 1-0. This type of excessively low pressure is referred to as a bunker. And when you're severely outmatched in talent, it makes sense.
- When you are protecting a lead, especially late in the game, you certainly don't want the game to open up. A team that high presses can get stretched out, and that's a recipe for conceding goals. Moving to a low-pressure system when you're holding onto a lead helps to keep your team compact and defensively organized. It also limits the space behind your line of defenders, which among other things, helps to neutralize the speed of the opposing forwards.
At this point I should mention that a low-pressure defense isn't synonymous with a well-organized defense. One doesn't automatically equal the other. Playing low pressure ensures that you'll get more bodies

behind the ball, but not much else. Bodies behind the ball is a good thing, but it's not the only thing; it's just a starting point. It's up to you to organize those bodies and to teach them to defend as a unit.

- When fatigue is a consideration, a low-pressure system can be a wise choice. Maybe you are low on subs, or it's scorching hot, or it's your third game in two days – any circumstance that has you concerned about the energy level of your players may be a time to opt for a low-pressure system. It eliminates a lot of the chasing you would do in a high-pressure set. Incidentally, if you plan on being one of those relentless, press-at-all-cost teams, your players better be darn fit and you'd better have an assembly line of soldiers ready to come off your bench. You can't expect two or three forwards to run like banshees for an entire match.

- So far I may have given you the impression that high pressure should be your first choice with low pressure being a timely alternative, but the fact of the matter is that some teams are just better off playing in a low pressure set-up. I think this particularly true for a team of average ability that just happens to have a track star or two up front. You invite your opponent into your end and then try to quickly counter into the space behind their defense.

A team that plays a well-organized, low-pressure defense can be very difficult to figure out. That's especially true in the U.S. because almost every youth-level team uses high pressure as its default system of defending. Very few teams know how to deal with a low-pressure opponent because they almost never see them. When they encounter a team that knows how to sit in and counter, it can cause worlds of problems. I do feel that if you're going to opt for low-pressure as your go-to style, it is immensely helpful if you have some serious speed up top, even if every player on your team is technically gifted. The key to counterattacking is speed – getting the ball from one end of the field to the other in a hurry – and pure speed of foot goes a long way to creating danger on the counter.

6

Why High Pressure? (Part 2)

I've given you a few reasons why and when a high pressure set-up makes sense, but those were all tactical considerations. Now let me give you a philosophical one: *High pressure is what players want to do.* Kids want to run around with their hair on fire trying to impact the game. They see the ball, they want the ball, they run like mad to get the ball. It's what they're hard-wired to do and it's why every parent has had to endure watching that primitive brand of youth soccer we refer to as 'bumble bee soccer' where a pack of ten or more players swarms around the ball no matter where it goes. High pressure comes naturally; low pressure is more nuanced and takes a great deal of tactical savvy and discipline. High pressure is a much easier sell.

High pressure is about aggressively chasing the game to make something happen. There's no mystery to high pressure. It's very transparent. It's about imposing your will on the opponent with fearlessness of spirit – looking them in the eye and saying, "I'm coming after you for ninety minutes and at the end of the day we'll see who wins." That's the way kids want to play.

When you ask your team to back off and concede territory, it flies in the face of the competitive spirit. In a low-pressure system, you have to keep your players on a leash, and that's not why they signed up to play soccer. They play soccer so they can run around like lunatics in an effort to outcompete their opponents. I can make no better case for a high-pressure system of team defending than it just comes naturally to the American soccer player.

Now, all that said, I doubt there's a coach reading this book who needs to be sold on high pressure. Chances are you're reading this book because you want to learn how to do it better, and that's just fine. In spite of my rant on the value of high pressure, I'm not trying to convince you that high pressure is the best way or the right way or the only way for your team. And I don't think you should back away from teaching a low-pressure defense just because it's a tougher sell. As I mentioned earlier, I think every team should be able to move between at least two systems of defense, and some teams will be better off using low pressure as their default style. I'm just trying to convey the idea that kids will gravitate to high pressure over any other style, and you should use that to your advantage.

7

Words Matter

As a proponent of having more than one style of team defending in your pocket, I think you should know that words matter, and there are no words less inspiring in all of soccer than 'low pressure.' If you want to take the air out of your team's balloon, just announce that for the next game you're going to play low pressure.

Any coach who has ever tried to introduce low pressure to his team has probably had an experience like this: You've explained your objectives. You've gone over the players' roles. You've introduced a restraining line. Then, when the game starts (even if it's just an intra-squad scrimmage), the players suffer some type of community paralysis. The ball gets near them and they start to go after it, then they stop, then they start, then they stop. You can literally see them asking themselves, *"Should I go after it? Am I allowed to go after it? Will I get yelled at if I go after it?"* They take a step or two then suddenly halt and it looks like they walked into an electric fence. You're not sure what they're doing, but it doesn't look much like soccer, and it certainly doesn't look natural.

The problem is that players equate *high* and *low* with the intensity of our pressure as opposed to the area of the field where we will confront the ball. When a coach says *low pressure*, the players hear *no pressure*. I'm not kidding. That's a pretty fair translation.

As this is a book devoted to teaching high pressure defending, you may wonder why this even matters. Well, if you plan on introducing something other than high pressure to your team, you have to call it something. And if you've been referring to your primary style of defending as *high pressure*, then what are you going to call anything else, because if it isn't *high*, it must be *low*, yes? You see the trap we set for ourselves?

It's up to you to decide what lingo will work best for your team, but let me suggest an alternative: Just number your defensive sets. When you play without a restraining line, that's Pressure 1. Your next highest restraining line (say thirty-five yards from goal) is Pressure 2. If you set a restraining line at the top of the center circle, that's Pressure 3. Now when you go to training, you're not teaching high or low pressure, you're teaching Pressure 1, 2 or 3. It doesn't matter where your restraining line is, the players aren't hearing 'low pressure.' And during the course of a game, you can switch from one line to the next by holding up some fingers.

Is this really important? Maybe. Maybe not. But before you pass judgment, go tell your players you want to play low pressure and see how they react.

8

DANGER - The Ball in Behind

As mentioned earlier, the opponent's ball in behind your last defender is the single greatest threat to a high-pressure system. Maximizing the space between your line of defenders and your goalkeeper makes you naturally susceptible to quick-strike counterattacks. This doesn't mean that you shouldn't set up in high pressure or that doing so will automatically cause you to concede goals. You can make allowances for the inherent risk of playing high pressure, and you're going to have to make those allowances if you want to play it successfully.

When we think high pressure, we tend to think about forwards churning up a wake of dirt and grass as they pursue and harass opposing defenders. But that's only the front end of high pressure. What we do at the back end is equally important. The opponent will, from time to time, break our pressure. There's no getting around it – that's just soccer. When the opponent breaks pressure, we need our back end organized to deal with the threat.

22

Keep in mind that oftentimes our line of defenders is pushed up to midfield or beyond when the opponent breaks pressure. The space behind our defenders is as big as it's going to get, and that's what makes our team so vulnerable. Shrinking that space as quickly as possible is our objective, and we need to shrink it from both ends.

The big ball in behind your defenders only works if the ball actually gets in behind your defenders *and* simultaneously cuts your goalkeeper out of the equation. Both of those things need to happen for that ball to work. So how do we counter the counter?

We start by not allowing the opponent to play over the top of us. Our defenders need to read pressure on the ball and read service. If it looks like the opponent can play over the top of us, our defenders need to drop off in a hurry. If done well enough, the intended ball-over-the-top doesn't actually clear our line of defenders. Ideally one of those defenders can get his head on the ball to halt the attack.

I cannot possibly overstate how important this is. Defenders have to understand those times when they need to get on their horse and retreat to protect the space behind them. As someone who has coached a lot of games for a team set up to high press, I've suffered through my fair share of fatal counterattacks, and the vast majority of those counters were the result of a defender who didn't drop off quickly enough. That player didn't recognize that the opponent had broken pressure and, instead of dropping off, she stood rooted near midfield for a half-second too long. Before she knew it, that ball was flying over her head and the opponent was off to the races. If you're going to be effective at high pressure, it can't be just about your attacking players; it also has to be about your defenders knowing when it's time to turn tail and retreat. If your defenders can't get a handle on this concept, your team is going to bleed goals.

In addition to defenders who know when to drop off, your cause will be helped mightily by a goalkeeper who understands when to come forward...

way forward… like sweeper-keeper, out-of-the-eighteen forward. While our defenders are shrinking the space from front to back, our goalkeeper needs to capitalize on chances to shrink that space from back to front. This is particularly crucial when our line of defenders hasn't retreated far enough. A ball that clears our defensive line will be running away from opposing forwards but running towards our goalkeeper. This gives our goalkeeper the opportunity to preempt potentially dangerous attacks from our opponent by moving forward and operating as an eleventh field player.

Do not underestimate the impact of a goalkeeper who affects the game in this manner. In addition to his practical effectiveness in dismantling attacks, he also poses a very frustrating challenge for the opposing side. When the opponent has a chance to escape pressure and spring a forward in behind the defense with an early ball, the player making that killer pass likely isn't factoring the goalkeeper into the equation. In his mind, he's caught the defensive line too high and sees a chance to play a teammate in behind the defense, so he's just knocking the ball into the open space intending for the forward to run onto it. An aggressive goalkeeper can often be first to that ball and eradicate the attack before it becomes dangerous. What seemed like Breakaway City a moment earlier becomes just another busted play. When a team repeatedly fails to solve this puzzle, it becomes a demoralizing proposition.

This type of active goalkeeping begins with a goalkeeper who takes up an aggressive starting position. When it comes to balls that get behind our defense, my advice to goalkeepers has always been this: *If you can get to the ball first, go!* Racing out of the goal area doesn't come naturally to a lot of goalkeepers. Stepping out of the eighteen is like entering a haunted forest for some of them, and they'd just prefer to stay near the goal, nestled in the safety of their little cocoon. Thankfully, most 'keepers can be trained to take that leap for the greater good. Your job is to convince them that if they can win the race to the ball, then that's exactly what they should do.

Now, if we're going to ask our goalkeeper to win some races, we want him to have as big of a head start as possible. So here is my second piece of advice to goalkeepers: *Play as far forward as you can without the opponent being able to knock a ball over your head.* So, if the ball is down near the opponent's eighteen, I'd like my 'keeper a solid thirty-five yards out in front of the goal. If he goes much further than that, a ball that gets bombed beyond the defenders might also get beyond the goalkeeper. Additionally, if the goalkeeper moves too far forward, he starts to crowd the back four which eliminates his effectiveness as a negative passing option for those players. Thirty-five yards is a comfortable middle ground that will allow the goalkeeper to sweep up behind the defenders while also preserving his integrity as a safety-valve passing option.

Some goalkeepers can be easily persuaded to take up an aggressive starting spot, but as soon as the ball looks like it might be headed toward their end, they scurry back toward their hole like a fiddler crab. It's no good to take up an aggressive starting position if you're just going to surrender it at the first sign of danger. I want my goalkeeper's first instinct to be forward not backward. Remember, the objective is to be first to a ball that gets past the defenders, and that usually means you have to come forward to do so.

Advanced goalkeepers – ones who can read the play – will hang on to their starting spot for as long as prudent. They'll find a balance between holding that spot and retreating only as far as necessary. And of course, sometimes that does in fact mean retreating all the way back to the goal. My point is: If you're going to clean up behind the back four, you've got to give yourself the best possible chance to be first to the ball.

An aggressive goalkeeper is a big time problem-solver for a team that's pressing high. He can cut out a lot of the balls that find their way past the defenders. He can take a promising counterattack and smash it into smithereens. He's like an extra defender who magically materializes out of thin air at just the right time to eliminate the threat and extinguish our opponent's hope.

Remember, for the ball in behind to be effective, it has to clear your line of defenders *and* cut out the goalkeeper. If your goalkeeper is good with his feet and mobile out of his eighteen, he will take care of a lot of problem balls that land behind your back four. If you try to play high pressure with a goalkeeper who is anchored to his line, you'd better hope he's darn good at stopping break-aways, because he's going to see a lot of them. To truly take care of your back end in high pressure, you need a goalkeeper who is willing to move forward to clean up that space behind the back four.

9

Restraining Lines

This term has come up often enough already so it's about time we attach some type of definition to it.

As your team sets into its defensive shape, your ten field players form a defensive block. This block is what the opponent must penetrate to advance the ball up the field.

When we talk about a system of pressure – high or low – we are talking about the area of the field where the highest attacking players will set up to initiate their defensive duties once the opponent achieves possession of the ball. If the forwards are persistently chasing the ball deep in the opponent's end of the field, they are pressing up high, and thus are operating in a high-pressure system. If those forwards instead retreat to midfield and wait for the opponent to engage, they are playing in a very low-pressure system.

In soccer terms, a restraining line is where your highest players will confront the ball as the opponent moves it toward your end of the field. It's important to recognize that as your forwards wait at their restraining line, they'll rarely be challenging the opponent's forwards. In other words, if you set your restraining line at midfield and I'm an opposing forward, I'm not likely to challenge your ten-man defensive block with a solo dribble. Typically when a forward is confronting a ball-carrier at the restraining line, that ball carrier is an opposing defender.

When you watch a televised game and you're trying to figure out what type of pressure a team is set up to play, it's the forwards who will give you that information. They are the ones dictating the restraining line. The players behind them work off the forwards' cues.

Incidentally, restraining lines aren't necessarily rigid. Don't think of a restraining line as a fence, but more like a swimming pool rope that's got some give to it. If a team plays a restraining line at midfield, the player who confronts the ball will typically move out across the restraining line once the ball is within eight or ten yards of midfield.

Restraining Line

In this diagram, the restraining line is set at midfield. The forward prepares to confront the ball as the opposing defender advances toward the restraining line. Moving the defensive block back like this decreases the space between the defenders and the goalkeeper and allows the defenders to set the offside line. It also draws the opponent's back line away from their goal, creating a potentially dangerous counter-attacking space.

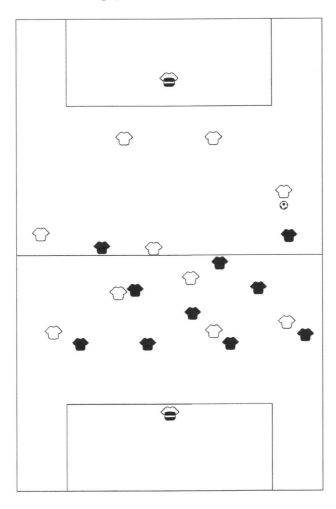

10

The High Restraining Line

In the purest form of high pressure, there is no restraining line. Wherever the ball goes, players move in to pressure. But that doesn't mean you can't play a high-pressure system and not also incorporate a restraining line. They aren't mutually exclusive. For example, you can set your restraining line 35 yards in front of the opponent's goal and still play in a high pressure system.

If we're combining pure high pressure with a restraining line, it's likely that we're dealing with some type of dead-ball situation. In other words, we drop to our restraining line if the opponent has a goal kick, a free kick inside or near its eighteen, or if the opponent's goalkeeper has the ball in hand. The idea is to discourage the opponent from playing over the top of our first layer. Instead, we invite them to play underneath our forwards. If, for example, we set a restraining line forty yards in front of the opponent's goal, that restraining line becomes pretty irrelevant if the goalkeeper punts the ball sixty yards down the field. At that point our restraining line moves our forwards closer to where the ball will return to Earth, and there's definitely a value to that when it comes to winning the second ball, but it does nothing to set up our initial press.

One of the reasons to set up a restraining line in a high-pressure set is to bait the opponent into putting the ball on the ground close to their goal. If the opposing goalkeeper is willing to roll the ball out or take a short goal kick, our restraining line invites that decision. Our hope is that as the goalkeeper distributes to a defender, we immediately move in to press.

If the opponent is willing to put the ball on the ground in front of your forwards, your challenge is to figure out exactly how high you can set your forwards without scaring the opponent out of repeating that behavior. In other words, you want to see how high you can keep your line while still enticing the opponent to put the ball on the ground. If the goalkeeper will roll the ball out when your forwards are only twenty-five yards off the end-line, well then there's no point in dropping off to thirty yards.

Obviously this master plan hinges on your opponent's style of play. Your forwards could drop off to midfield when the opposing goalkeeper gets the ball in her hands, but that won't guarantee that she won't punt it anyway. However, if your opponent fancies itself as a possession team, you may be able to bait them into putting the ball on the deck in front of your forwards. This is the dream scenario for a high-pressure restraining line.

High Restraining Line 1

In this diagram, the goalkeeper has the ball and the pressing team has re-treated to its restraining line. The idea is to entice the goalkeeper into playing underneath our forwards.

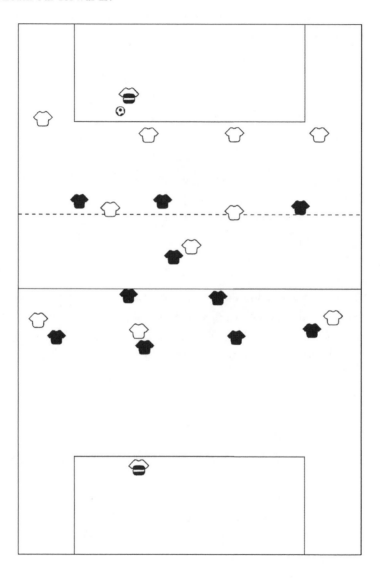

High Restraining Line 2

Once the goalkeeper distributes the ball, the opponent quickly moves into press. To keep the layers connected, the line of defenders is sprinting to mid-field, forcing the opposing strikers back toward their own goal which further condenses the space. Part of the pressing forward's job is to arrive quickly enough to eliminate a big ball over the top. Even the goalkeeper pushes further up the field to patrol the space behind the line of defenders.

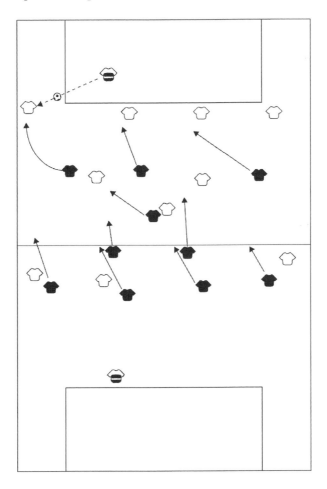

11

Breaking Pressure

B *reaking pressure* is a term we'll be referring to quite often, and it's the most important cue in determining when it's time to discontinue your press, retreat and regroup.

Let's consider a scenario where the opponent is in possession in its defensive third. Their left back has the ball and your players are working hard to put pressure on the ball and take away short options. You have good numbers around the ball so you have a reasonable chance of dispossessing the opponent. At this point the opponent is under pressure.

Then the left back slips a pass in to a center midfielder who quickly switches the ball to the unpressured right midfielder. The opponent has successfully played its way out of your pressure. In other words, they broke pressure. And now you need an exit strategy.

When the opponent breaks pressure, it's time to shift gears mentally and physically and move on to Plan B. There's likely no point in chasing that outlet pass at a full sprint because there is so much ground to cover. To have a team full of players sprinting from one side of the field to the other is just a waste of effort. It's impossible to sustain that effort for very long and you'll just end up with a bunch of exhausted players. So instead of chasing in the wake of the ball, your players angle their runs back and to the ball-side of the field in an attempt to get numbers behind the ball. Once they get behind the ball they can regroup into a cohesive defensive shape.

A high-pressure system involves a lot of chasing from your forwards. But there's a time to chase and there's a time to back off and get numbers behind the ball. When the opponent clearly breaks pressure, it's time to back off. The ability of all players to recognize this is essential to organized team defending. Regardless of where you confront the ball, you want to defend in a pack. Players who chase when they should retreat separate themselves from their teammates, stretching out your team's defensive shape (think of the bowling pins).

Even if your team is exceptional at pressing up high, there will still be times when the opponent breaks pressure. That's just soccer. It happens. In those moments, we don't want our players killing themselves to force an untenable situation. Don't take a small problem and turn it into a bigger one. When the opponent breaks pressure, it's time to cut our losses and live to fight another day. Instead of trying to force a bad situation, just retreat, get numbers behind the ball, get organized and defend as a unit. If our initial pressure fails, we simply need to retreat and regroup and find a new opportunity to win the ball.

12

The Pawn

In spite of everything you read in the last chapter, oftentimes, when the opponent is just about to break your pressure, it's wise to sacrifice a pawn. This
is one of those topics that would be much easier to explain with video, but since
that isn't an option, I'll do my best to paint the picture with words.

Let's begin with the simple premise that when our team is pushed into the
attacking half of the field, that's when we are the most vulnerable to a quick
counterattack. One common characteristic of a quick counterattack is a big,
early ball forward. Therefore, when the opponent is about to break pressure, it
is in our best interest to deny them the opportunity to play that vertical pass.
The more passes it takes for the opponent to build its attack, the more time
our team has to recover into a defensive shape, and the more time our line of
defenders has to retreat to protect the space in behind them. Any pass the opponent plays that is short or square or negative buys our team more time to defend.

When the opponent is in the process of breaking pressure, your priorities
need to shift from pressing to damage control. In other words, if we can't do
the best thing – winning the ball back immediately, then we need to do the

second-best thing – preventing the opponent from connecting a long, vertical pass.

Let's say that your team is enjoying a sustained attack deep in the opponent's territory and you've got players bombing forward when suddenly a pass gets deflected and the ball is about to end up at the opposing center back. At that point your team is at its most vulnerable and the immediate objective is to keep the opponent from advancing the ball with its first pass. This moment often requires a player to chase after a lost cause just to prevent the opponent from playing vertically.

Once the center back receives the ball, you know that he's got enough space and enough options that your pressure will be broken. At that point it's no longer about pressing to dispossess; it's about pressing to subdue. Even if you know that you can't win the ball directly, you want to take away the thing that will do the most harm and make him do something less damaging. The ball forward – particularly the big, early ball forward – is the biggest threat to your team. It can eliminate six or seven of your players, maybe more, with one swing of the axe. That's why it's critical to prevent the opponent from playing a long, vertical ball as its first pass out of pressure.

So let's go back to the opposing center back who is about to receive the ball near the top of his eighteen and break our pressure. Let's say I'm playing left wing for our team, and I recognize that pressure is about to be broken. I also recognize that when the center back receives the ball, he's potentially going to have an opportunity to pick up his head and play that big ball forward. If I pressure him quickly enough, I can take away that option, but to do so means that I'm going to give him a very easy escape hatch to play a square ball to his right back who will be completely unpressured. So what do I do?

In this situation, the answer is to concede the square ball in order to prevent the vertical one. As pressure is being broken, my teammates should begin retreating. By forcing the center back to play laterally, I'm buying my teammates a few more seconds to get back behind the ball and consolidate into a defensive block, and I'm giving my line of defenders the chance to retreat. Even though I am pulling myself away from my teammates and away from our defensive block, it's a good trade. I have to give myself up as the sacrificial pawn for the greater good. So I sprint to pressure the center back knowing full well I won't win the ball from him, but also knowing that if I can force him to play laterally, the chances of a quick counterattack virtually disappear.

These moments often require a player to chase after a lost cause just to prevent the opponent from playing vertically. If we can force that first pass to be a square one (or better yet, a negative one), we typically cripple the attempt at a quick counter. Your players need to understand the value of delaying the opponent's forward progress in the moments following a loss in possession.

The ability to force something other than a vertical pass requires immediate recognition from a player close to the ball who can arrive at an angle that shuts down the vertical seam. That's the player who has to sacrifice himself for the big picture. He's the player who may have to sprint forward while all his teammates are retreating.

Later we'll discuss putting immediate pressure on the ball after we've lost possession, but that will be geared more toward winning back possession. This is different. This is about choosing the lesser of two evils when we know possession will not be regained. The opponent is definitely going to have a way out; we just want to make sure he takes the way that does the least amount of damage. Any way you slice it, the longer it takes the opponent to advance the ball vertically, the better off we'll be.

13

Staying Connected

When you press, it is critical that you hunt in packs. To do that, you need to keep your back connected to your front, and your left connected to your right. If you don't, your blanket rips.

Think of each row of your players as a layer. The forwards are the first layer. The midfielders are the second. The defenders are the third and the goalkeeper is the fourth. The more space there is between those layers, the easier it is for the opponent to operate with the ball. When those spaces get too big, there are holes in our blanket.

Let's say the ball and all twenty field players are in our half of the field. Then someone clears the ball into the opponent's end of the field towards the corner of their eighteen. The opposing left back will be the first one to the ball. Our forwards recognize that this is a good time to chase because the left back will be facing his own corner flag when he catches up to the ball. So our forwards sprint to put pressure on the ball. Immediately our layer of forwards is separating itself from our layer of midfielders, unless our midfielders also recognize the situation and also sprint to support the forwards. So as our midfielders sprint forward, they are separating themselves from the layer of defenders, unless of course that layer is also moving ahead at the same pace as the forwards and midfielders.

When the first forward arrives to pressure the ball, it's critical to understand that he might not be the player who actually wins the ball. Oftentimes, he won't be the one winning it. But he is going to make the opposing player's life difficult. Now let's say the opposing player turns just enough to attempt a pass to his defensive center midfielder. This is really where the rubber meets the road. If our second layer has stayed connected to the first layer, there's an excellent chance that we might win the ball. But if our second layer is late to the party, the opponent is going to break pressure.

It's been my experience that the second layer arriving a little bit late might actually be worse than it not really arriving at all. Let's stay with the same example – the left back plays in to the defensive center mid. Our center mid is late by a step or two, but not late enough that he still doesn't attempt to put in a tackle. So as he goes flying at the ball, the opponent makes a forward pass to the attacking center mid. Now our first and second layers have both been eliminated. If our center mid knew he was going to be late, he could've just put on the brakes, sat a little deeper and stalled the opponent, keeping our defensive block of eight or nine players intact. Instead he pressed a bad situation and got himself eliminated and now the opponent is through two of our three layers. When the supporting layers are late, a good team will tic-tac-toe its way through the gaps between the layers.

Keeping the layers connected is critical to organized pressure, and it's not just so one layer can support the layer in front of it. It also works in the other direction. If the layers are in close enough proximity, a player can work back to support the layer behind him. Let's say our right wing is pressing on the opposing left back. That left back slips a pass into the defensive center mid. If our layers are close enough, this might be a great opportunity for our center forward to work back to double-team the player on the ball. But that won't happen if he has to run twenty yards to do it. We need to keep our layers tight.

In a high-pressure system, it's important that the goalkeeper also stay connected. As the line of defenders moves up the field, so should the goalkeeper. Now he won't stay as close to the defenders as the defenders stay to the midfielders, but it is important that he move above his eighteen as the ball moves deep into opposition territory. He has to have the courage to move forward to cut out a threat. Remember, when you are pressing high up the field, you are most vulnerable because of the space that develops between your goalkeeper and your defenders. Your goalkeeper must do his part to patrol that space, and he must be willing to aggressively move forward to clean up balls that get in behind the defenders.

When the moment comes to press high up the field, it's often a forward who will lead the charge. If he's chosen a good time to press, it's up to his teammates to follow suit. A good rule of thumb is that when one goes, we all go!

One way to address this concept at training is to play an 11v11 scrimmage with the restriction that, to score, all field players on the attacking team must be in the opponent's half of the field. This forces both teams into a high-pressure style, which opens up the space behind the defenders and leads to quick counterattacks. Those counterattacks force the second and third layers to sprint up the field, and that in turn keeps all the layers connected.

The real benefit of this game isn't when those quick counterattacks lead to a goal, but rather when the opponent stymies the counter and wins back possession deep in its own territory. Now the team that launched the counter has its layers connected in the opponent's half and is in an excellent position to press up high.

Staying connected isn't just about your vertical layers; it's equally important that your horizontal layers also move in unison. In a high-pressure set, we're going to gamble positionally to shrink the field. To do that, we're going to give away the weak side. In other words, if we are pressing the opponent's left back, the player we are least concerned about — at least temporarily — is the opponent's right wing because we know the player on the ball can't deliver a pass to that particular teammate. Similarly, if we are in a three-front for example, as we press the left back, our own left wing will pinch in towards the center of the field and abandon the opponent's right back. When we gamble like this, we are basically daring the ball-carrier to attempt a pass to the players we are leaving unguarded because the risk is high and the chances of success are low. To produce effective high pressure, we need to get numbers around the ball, and to do that, we need our weak-side players gravitating to the ball-side of the field. I'll oversimplify this by saying that our players should move like they're on a Foosball rod. When you push that rod to one side of the field, all the players move in unison to that side.

Let's say you're playing a three-front and the time has come to press high up the field on your attacking left side. Your center forward and left wing are busting their tails to pressure the ball, but your right wing is hanging out near her sideline, tightly marking the left back. The opponent escapes up the alley between your right wing and your center forward because your horizontal layers didn't stay connected, and now you have two very aggravated attackers because all their hard work was for naught.

When teaching team defense, whether its high pressure or low pressure or anything in between, it's important that your players understand the difference between position and positioning. This is particularly evident for wide players. Although their titles may begin with 'left' or 'right', the game will often dictate that they abandon the flanks and move into centralized positions. This can be a struggle for players who've never received much advanced coaching. A player who has spent eight years being told he's a left wing, mainly because he's fast and left-footed, has been conditioned to hug the sideline and only worry about defending the opposing right back. He's been groomed as a left wing. Now you've got to persuade him to move centrally when the ball is on the far side of the field. You've got to show him the difference between position and positioning. That's the only way to shrink the field so your team can hunt in packs.

High pressure can't work if the entire team doesn't stay connected from back to front and from side to side. It can't be accomplished by a couple of freelancers. You have to commit numbers to the ball and make a crowded space. Everybody has to be on board. It has to be a community project and every player has to pull her own weight.

Ripped Blanket

In this diagram, the first two layers (forwards and midfielders) have stepped up to put pressure on the ball, but the third layer is slow to join them. A large gap forms between the second and third layers. This is an excellent space for the opponent to receive the ball.

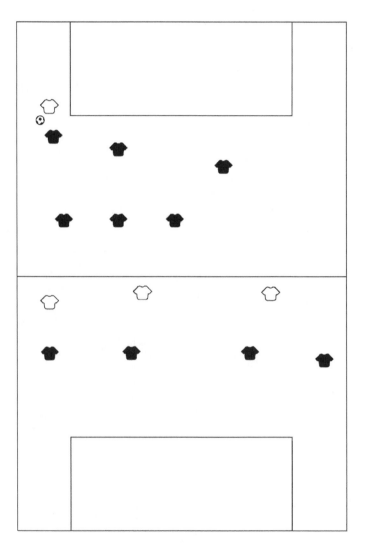

14

No Free Outs

To be effective at high pressure, your team must be able to lock down the opponent in its own end. I'll say this a lot, but oftentimes it is not the pressing forwards who will win the ball for your team. Oftentimes it is the work of those forwards that will force an imperfect pass or an imperfect clearance that becomes the turnover, and that change in possession will often happen near midfield. In those instances, your defender who wins the ball is the beneficiary of the forward's pressure.

A large percentage of goals scored during the run of play in a soccer match are the result of three or fewer passes. About half the goals scored during the run of play begin when the ball is won within 40 yards of the opponent's goal. Think about that for a moment: For all the time we spend working on possession, goals are typically the result of winning the ball in the opponent's defensive third and then driving immediately to goal. That's a pretty strong case for high pressure.

When the opponent gains possession close to their own goal, they either break pressure or they don't. Regardless of how hard our forwards are working to get pressure on the ball, oftentimes it's the play of our back four that determines whether or not the opponent escapes. The ability of our back four to prevent the opponent from escaping out of its defensive third is a critical element for turning high-pressure defense into goal-scoring chances. If our defenders win that battle, at the very least we keep the opponent locked in. At best, the resurgence of pressure leads to a goal. This is the quintessential example of turning high-pressure defense into attack. The defenders bend the branch so the attackers can pick the fruit.

In this chapter, we're going to discuss instances when the ball is deep in the opponent's end of the field and the opponent's forwards are on their side of the midfield stripe. Just to paint a clearer picture, let's assume the opponent is playing with three forwards.

Let's begin with a simple premise: A forward who can hold the ball with her back to pressure is a tremendous asset to her team. She is the escape hatch. If she can be first to a clearance and protect the ball, her teammates will move up the field to build the attack. Therefore it stands to reason that it is in our own best interest not to allow the opposing forwards to hold the ball.

Eliminating the target forward as an option for an outlet pass is one of the most important things a defense can do in the war for territory. It often determines whether or not the opponent breaks pressure. If your team does this well, you'll be very difficult to beat.

I referred to our mission to prevent forwards from holding the ball as *No Free Outs*. That meant that no forward should be allowed to hold or even receive the ball with her back to pressure in her own half of the field. When that forward checked back to the ball, our objective was to get there first. Here are some tips to accomplish the objective:

Don't Guard the Midfield Stripe — You can see this all the time at the youth level. The forwards will be ten yards into their own half of the field while the opposing defenders are anchored at midfield like they'll be electrocuted if they advance any further. When we have the opponent pinned deep in their end, we want to keep them there. Playing too loose on the forwards makes their job easy. It makes it easy for them to be first to the clearances; it makes it easy for them to hold the ball, and it makes it easy for them to turn the ball.

My philosophy was that in these situations, we were going to gamble. We were dead set on squishing the field from back to front. Our backs were going to be so tight on the checking wingers that we were going to dare teams to play over the top of us. If the outlet ball came to a checking winger, our objective was to jump the pass and be first to the ball. The same thing applied to our center backs if it was the center forward checking back. We were going to over-play the pass underneath us and invite the opponent to hit it over the target's head. If they played over the top of us, it was a deeper defender's responsibility to win the ball.

Cheating – Defenders are taught to always stay goal-side because that keeps them between the player they are marking and the goal. That's pretty sound advice but sometimes we can do better. What if, instead of starting behind the checking attacker, we started beside her? Wouldn't that give us a better chance to be first to the ball? Of course it would. So let's start looking for opportunities to cheat.

When you're expecting a clearance, read the player on the ball and assess her chances of actually clearing you, or even reaching you, with her clearance. If you don't think her clearance can reach you in the air, then there's no point in waiting behind the attacker.

Many years ago I ran a test with my defenders. The defenders and I started 15 yards in front of the end-line. I rolled a ball toward the end-line. Each defender would have to sprint to the ball as fast as she could, spin and hit a one-touch clearance over my head before the ball rolled out of bounds. Would you believe that 90% of those clearances never even got shoulder high? The vast majority came in at waist-height! So what's the point in standing 40 yards away from the ball when it's only going to cover 25 yards in the air?

If you can read that the opponent clearing the ball is going to struggle to reach her target, move from goal-side to alongside the target, and as soon as she makes contact with the ball, jump in front of the player you're marking and try to be first to the ball.

Anytime a defender can be first to a ball that targets a forward near midfield, it's an opportunity to keep the opponent locked in and to turn the screws a little tighter. Conversely, if we allow the opponent's target to receive and hold the ball, our high pressure won't be very effective.

When teaching high pressure, it's easy to get fixated on the work and positioning of the forwards near the opponent's goal. You have to remember that many critical battles will be won near midfield.

15

Plus One

If you play with a back four and you are actively pressing the opponent deep in their end, you obviously want to keep them locked in for as long as possible, or at least until you force a turnover. To do that, you need to commit numbers to the ball side of the field.

When you have a forward working hard to press an opposing defender in the wide corridor of the field, it's important that your ball-side, outside back presses up to the fray. The ball-side, outside back is often the player who will destroy or intercept the outlet pass that would otherwise break your pressure. For example, if you're pressing the right back along the sideline, and that player connects a pass to the right wing who can hold the ball, then there's an excellent chance your pressure has been broken. As we discussed in the last chapter, I wanted my outside backs to gamble. I wanted them playing right beside – not behind – the opposing winger. I wanted them to take away the ball underneath. I wanted them to dare the opponent to play over the top. Now, they still had to read the body language of the player on the ball and drop off if it looked like she was going to whack a ball over the top, but I definitely did not want my outside backs to concede the pass into the winger's feet. If the ball was played to the winger's feet, I wanted my outside backs to be first to the ball. Even if that winger dropped back to her own eighteen, I wanted the outside back to go with her.

To balance out the defense, if the left back was pushed up, the right back would hold back a bit. If the ball suddenly moved to our right side of the field, the right back would press up and the left back would balance back.

That's pretty easy to understand when the ball is in a wide corridor, but what if it's in the central corridor? If the ball was in the central corridor of the field, the outside backs couldn't gamble quite so much territorially. I didn't want one big ball to eliminate two of my four defenders, so they had to be a little less committal until they saw where the ball was going. Still, if one of them read that the next ball would be aimed for the winger's feet, she would gamble forward to try to keep the opponent locked in.

One of the great mistakes defenders make when their team is pressing high is to stand sentry on the midfield stripe like it's an electric fence that can't be crossed. I didn't want my defenders tethered to midfield if they had a chance to help our cause. To hammer home this philosophy, I introduced the Plus One rule. The Plus One rule simply states that for however many attackers the opponent would leave up near midfield, we would make sure we would have a plus one advantage – and *not more* than plus one. I didn't want to look across the midfield stripe and see the opposing center forward standing on the center spot as the lone, high attacker, and then see my four defenders anchored to midfield. That's just two wasted players serving as spectators. If they had one player standing at midfield, then we would have two – one to mark that player and the other to serve as back-up. If they had two, we would have three, but never more than plus one unless we were trying to close out a win.

Plus One – Wide Corridor

In this example, the ball is in a wide corridor of the field and the left back has pushed up to challenge a retreating winger while the right back balances back into a defensive shape.

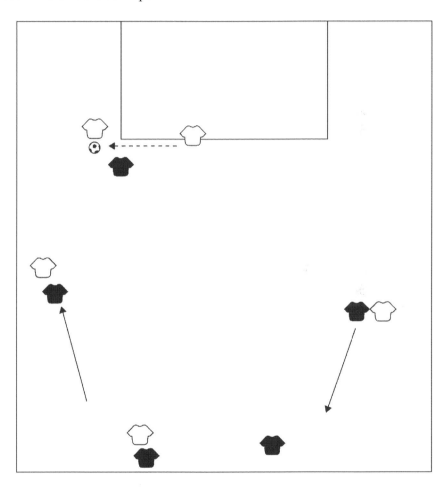

Plus One – Central Corridor

In this diagram, the ball is in a central corridor and both outside backs hold back a bit, waiting to see where the ball will go next.

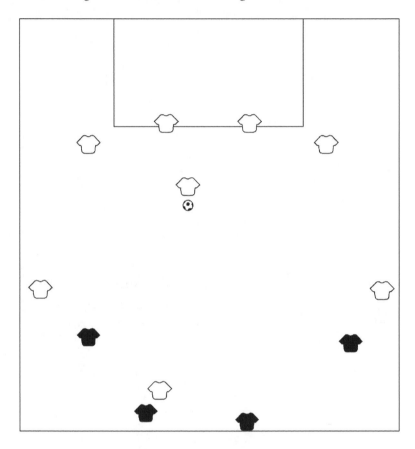

16

Cues

There's a time to press up high, a time to be patient, and a time to pull up stakes and retreat. Recognizing when to do which is the difference between an effective press and a waste of energy. When it comes to pressing, you need to pick your moments. So, when exactly is a good time to move into a pressing mode high up the field? Well, the short answer is anytime it will cause problems for the opposition. A smart pressing team will recognize those moments when stepping on the gas will likely inflict maximum difficulty. Here are a few good cues:

Immediately after we turn over the ball. When our team has possession of the ball, the opponent will naturally fall into a compact defensive shape. The closer we get to their goal, the more compact that shape will become. At the moment they win the ball, they are still in that shape, bunched closely together. As they hold possession, they begin to spread out and expand into an attacking shape, and winning back possession becomes more difficult. As soon as we recognize possession is *about to be lost*, that's an excellent time to step up into a pressing mode to force the issue before the opponent has the opportunity to expand into an attacking shape. If we can immediately pressure the ball, there's an excellent chance we can win it back before the opponent connects a single pass. The closer the ball is to the opponent's goal, the more important this is because our chances of success will be higher. The opponent will never be as tightly bunched as when we are threatening their goal. This is when it will take them the most time to expand into an attacking shape. By that same token, the opponent doesn't want to mess around with the ball close to its goal, so immediate pressure often results in a panicked attempt at a clearance.

We can even break this concept down further to focus not solely upon the opponent's team shape, but also upon the individual opponent who has gained possession. This player has made some type of move for the ball. Now sometimes that player has already figured out what to do with the ball before it has arrived and can quickly play himself out of trouble. But oftentimes, because he's had to react to the ball and has put his head down to make the play, he is starting from scratch. He wins the ball and then begins the process of evaluating his options. This is a player we want to get after as quickly as possible, before he has mapped out a good option.

Barcelona has become world soccer darlings for its ability to connect passes, but if you pay attention, they are also a fantastic pressing team. You may have heard of Barcelona's 'six-second rule,' which basically states that when they lose the ball, they will make a concerted team effort to win the ball back within six seconds. When Barcelona loses possession, it suddenly looks like a fire drill as the players rush to put immediate pressure on the ball and win it back. Their commitment to immediately pressuring the ball makes it very difficult for opponents to get their shape to start an attack.

It's also interesting to note that if Barcelona hasn't won the ball back in six seconds, the players will retreat and form up behind the ball. The six-second rule is one way they gauge whether or not pressure has been broken.

When a defender has to chase down a ball while she's facing her own goal. If we can get pressure on her back that prevents her from turning, we have the chance to give her a difficult problem to solve and we don't want to let her off the hook. This is particularly true if we have the opportunity to cut out the goalkeeper as a viable passing option. Most of the time, if an outside back has to chase a ball back toward her corner flag, we have an opportune moment to press. Additionally, if the ball that a defender is chasing back toward her goal is in the air or bouncing, that defender is faced with a difficult technical challenge and it would be wise to put her under immediate pressure to force her into making a difficult play.

When you spot a long, soft or difficult pass. An opponent's under-hit pass can be an excellent cue to step up your pressure, simply because the pressuring player can make up ground while the ball is en route. The same can hold true for a long pass, such a flighted ball from the left back to the right back. While the ball is in the air, the first pressuring player can cover a lot of ground. Either way, if you can arrive at the destination at approximately the same time as the ball, you can put the receiving player in a very difficult spot. A clever pressuring player will also recognize when the pass will be difficult to handle. For example, if the pass is in the air, has pace and bend on it, and will bounce a few yards in front of the target – that's a difficult ball to bring under control and is a good cue to step up your pressure. If you think the receiving player will have trouble with her first touch, you don't want to give her the luxury of a second touch.

A Bad First Touch. Even if the pass doesn't appear difficult to receive, that's no guarantee that the receiving player won't take a bad first touch. A touch that gets away from the receiving player can signal an opportunity to shift into a higher pressing gear. When we press, we want to be unforgiving of technical mistakes.

An opponent's throw-in deep in their own end. Not many players can throw the ball in further than twenty yards. That number is even smaller on the girl's side. Unless the opponent has a long throw, they're going to have to work their way out of a difficult spot if you press. Even if you're playing a low-pressure system, this is still a good cue to step up and press until the opponent solves the problem.

When you identify a weak link. If there is a player on the opposing team who is technically inept, particularly a defender, it makes sense to step up your pressure whenever that player is receiving the ball. That said, if your opponent is full of technically inept players, it gives you much more freedom to press at will.

A pass back to the goalkeeper. This is one that you'll have to handle on a case by case basis. If the center back turns at midfield and pings a pass back to her goalkeeper, there's no sense in having your center forward sprint after it if she can't get close enough to cause a problem before the 'keeper hoofs the ball sixty yards back up the field. However, a back-pass to the 'keeper might also be a wonderful invitation to step up your pressure, particularly if that pass is under-hit or difficult to receive or if it comes to the goalkeeper's weak foot. Sometimes we want to chase that pass simply to force the goalkeeper into launching a 50-50 clearance. If we're dominating the opponent in the air, those 50-50 balls may end up being 80-20 balls in our favor. If chasing the pass back to the goalkeeper will cause the opponent some type of uncomfortable disruption, your player should seriously consider making the effort.

When the goalkeeper distributes to a defender. Remember, you can have a restraining line and still high press. This is one of the oldest ways to arrange that marriage. The goalkeeper gets the ball in her hands and the opposing side retreats to its restraining line, thirty-five or forty yards in front of the goal. Their objective is to bait the goalkeeper into throwing out to one of the outside backs. When the 'keeper throws the ball, the pressing team immediately shifts into high gear to press.

A predetermined pass. Similar to the previous cue, some pressing teams will sit back at their restraining line and wait for the first square pass, or the first pass to an outside back, or the first pass from an outside back to a center back, or the first pass into a holding midfielder. It's just one more way to set the trap.

You allow the goalkeeper to distribute to a defender, but instead of going after the ball from the goalkeeper, you go after the next pass or whichever pass meets your pressing criteria. The idea is that your restraining line will induce the player on the ball to play a pass that isn't forward. As the ball comes off that player's foot, everyone moves into attack mode.

If you ask your team to chase everything everywhere at warp speed, your players are going to run out of gas in a hurry. You have to combine the physical effort with some cunning, and that hinges on the ability of your players to recognize the cues that invite pressing up high and to differentiate those cues from the stack of lost causes. It's critical that your forward-most players recognize the times to expend energy and the times to conserve it. As they typically lead the pressing charge, they are pulling the other layers along with them. Remember, *if one goes, we all go*, so we want to make sure that 'the one' knows what the heck she's doing. Otherwise we'll have a lot of players wasting a lot of energy.

17

Going Rogue

L et me give you a telltale sign of a smart pressing forward: He's the one who looks back at his teammates even as he is charging forward to press the opponent. Why is he glancing backwards? Because he wants to know, among other things, if his teammates are joining him. If they are nowhere to be found, he is smart enough to give up the chase and conserve his energy. There isn't a surplus of forwards with this type of soccer IQ, which is why a lot of hard work gets wasted. It's also why we need a brain in the midfield who can discern the right times to press from the wrong ones.

A high pressing system is greatly enhanced by a midfield general who recognizes the times to press and the times to sit back and organize. I can't possibly emphasize this enough. A player like that can run the show. He can encourage the attackers to push forward and press like he's commanding a team of sled dogs. He can also command those players to tap the brakes if he recognizes that the team is too disconnected to effectively press as a unit. There are times when a cue to press reveals itself but the team shape doesn't warrant a charge forward. If the cue is right but the shape is wrong, pressing isn't a sound choice. You need both pieces of the puzzle to press effectively, and that's one reason that a team trailing by one goal will end up losing by two. Late in the game, that team doesn't have the luxury of waiting for the right cue; they have to chase everything. That leads to breakdowns in team shape, gaps between the layers, and ultimately the nail-in-the-coffin counterattack.

A midfielder leader with a high soccer IQ and some leadership skills can effectively dictate a team's pressing tactics. He can push the forwards ahead of him and pull the defenders behind him. His voice can signal the time to go while keeping the team connected in the process. When that player shouts, "Let's go let's go let's go!," everyone knows it's time to commence the charge.

This player is also exceptionally valuable if one of your forwards chases unwisely. We've already established that if one goes, we all go. But what if the one gets it wrong? What if the one takes off on a suicide mission? Well, that player begins the painful process of stretching out your team shape, which is not at all what you want when the opponent has the ball. That player is putting stress on the fabric of your blanket. If even one more teammate joins him, the holes may start to appear.

If you have a midfield general who recognizes the mistake, he may be able to rein in the misguided forward. Maybe he starts shouting, "No Billy! Leave it!" And maybe that's enough to reel back his overzealous teammate. If the rogue forward ignores the command, your midfield general can still dissuade the rest of his teammates from joining the charge. If one forward goes rogue, it's not likely to be fatal. It'll certainly be a waste of energy, but it won't be catastrophic. However, the damage will be infinitely worse if other teammates join his cause. You're better off having one player making a mistake than ten players making that same mistake. A midfield general knows when to cut that forward loose and move into damage-control mode.

In this situation, when the opponent breaks pressure, which they will because they'll be playing six against one, the rogue forward will turn around and realize that his teammates have abandoned him. He'll realize that he just wasted a lot of energy and he won't be happy about it, but it will teach him to listen to the guy who's conducting the orchestra.

18

The First One In

Pressing up high demands a high work rate, especially from your forwards. They're the ones who set the tone and it's up to their teammates to keep up with the pace. It's not always a forward who is the first one to step up and press, but in the interests of simplicity, your reading pleasure, and my sanity, I'm just going to generalize this front-line role and stick with the term *forwards* as a catchall label for the first pressing players. Back to our story...

The player who initiates the pressure must do more than one job. His first job is to make play predictable. In other words, the angle of his approach must take something away from the player on the ball. More specifically, it must eliminate either the inside or the outside as a forward passing option. He has to steer the ball into an area where his teammates can do the most good. This approach sets up your pressing funnel, which we will discuss in a later chapter. If he does his job well, his teammates can begin making adjustments to strengthen the funnel. This is particularly important to his teammates in the second or third layers, as they will begin taking some positional risks in anticipation of where the opponent will play the next pass. Some of them will be asked to shift away from the opponent they are marking to shore up the funnel and force a turnover. To do this, they need to have confidence that the first player won't let the opponent on the ball out of the funnel.

Ideally, the angle of the first player's approach will eliminate one opponent as a close passing option. So let's say your funnel is set up to the inside. As your right wing moves to pressure the opponent's left back, hopefully he cuts out the opponent's left midfielder as an option. That won't always be the case if for no other reason than there won't always be a close passing option at that angle to cut out. But if there is, the pressing player should make every effort to take away that option as he begins his press.

Once he has made play predictable, his next job is to go after the ball with physical intensity. This is where a lot of forwards miss the boat. They do a good job of steering play into the funnel, but then they just stand there shadowing the opponent on the ball. In short, they defend like defenders. We teach our defenders to be patient when they are matched up 1v1 close to our goal. We coach them not to dive in after the ball. We tell them that it's the attacker's job to make something happen. We teach them to stall and wait for help. All of that makes perfect sense when you're defending close to your own goal because you have to be very cautious about the risks you take. So you stay patient and wait for the attacker to commit. That's not the intensity we're looking for at the other end of the field. Once the funnel is set, that first forward needs to *go after the ball*! He needs to limit the time the opponent has to get his head up and make a good decision. And he can afford to be a little bit reckless because if the opponent escapes his pressure, they are still ninety yards away from our goal. We don't want that forward being patient. We want him to gamble! We want him being aggressive in bringing the fight! Anything he can do to unbalance or unsettle the player on the ball helps our cause.

When the first presser is aggressive, the result is often a take-away from the second presser. So if the right wing goes flying in at the left back and the left back cuts the ball back toward the middle to escape the challenge, that touch might take the left back straight into a challenge from the center forward. As we'll discuss more in the next chapter, oftentimes it's not the first presser who actually wins the ball. Oftentimes it's the chaos he causes that results in a gift for one of his teammates.

Oftentimes, when the first player pressures an outside back, that defender will play to her near-side center back. Then the question becomes whether or not the first player should chase that pass. That's going to depend on a few factors, namely the distance and quality of the pass. Generally speaking, if that pass is fifteen yards or less, the forward should at least strongly consider chasing. But that's not the issue I want to discuss. I want to discuss what happens when the first player decides to chase that pass.

Too often, as that pass is made, the first forward will break off her initial pressuring run to chase the ball. It makes sense to take the shortest path, but too often, that forward doesn't cut off the player who made the initial pass.

So again, let's say our right wing is stepping to press the left back. The left back plays to the left center back and our right wing changes course to pursue the ball. As he steps to the center back, the center back simply returns the pass to the left back and our right wing has been eliminated.

When the right wing is pursuing that pass, he needs to do more than one job. He needs to take an angle of approach that cuts out the left back. As the ball leaves the left back's foot, it's going to travel in a straight line. Our right wing should take a path that's right along that line as if the ball was pulling him along by a string. This not only cuts out the return pass to the left back, but again it makes play predictable for his teammates. Incidentally, cutting off a short passing option isn't just true for the first pressing player; it's important for all players to recognize when they can eliminate a short passing option with the angle of their approach. When you cut off his options, the player on the ball is left to fend for himself. That frees up players to aggressively go after the ball and that often leads to turnovers.

I understand that this seems like simple common sense, but if you pay attention, you'll be amazed at how often the first player doesn't cut out the return pass. If the return pass is successful, the press usually collapses because your funnel sprung a giant leak. It's important to emphasize that all pressing players do more than one job whenever possible, but it's absolutely vital that the first player in accomplishes more than just running at the ball.

19

.

Selfless

The act of trying to regain possession immediately after you've lost it is known as counter-pressing, and it's a signature quality of effective high-pressure teams. The chance of your counter-press being successful largely hinges on two factors: How quickly you get pressure on the ball, and the shape of the opponent. The quicker you can pressure the ball, the more likely you are to force a turnover. Likewise, the more condensed the opponent's shape is when you lose possession, the more likely that your immediate pressure can cause them to cough up the ball.

As we've already discussed, the closer your team is to the opponent's goal when the ball is lost, the more condensed the opponent will be, and the more time it will take them to transition into an effective attacking shape. Therefore, it stands to reason that when you lose possession deep in the attacking third, your players should make an even greater effort to put immediate pressure on the ball. This is where the urgency and intensity we associate with high pressure should reveal itself. This is where we want to turn the game into pure pandemonium. The opponent has a serious problem and we want to do everything we can to compound it. When we have the opponent on the ropes, that's not the time to tap the brakes; that's the time to go in for the kill.

When our attack breaks down inside of the opponent's eighteen, our players typically make two mistakes. First, they take a second to wallow in their misfortune before making the effort to pressure the ball. Then, when they do pressure, they do it with something less than their very best effort. These are two epic blunders.

Remember this: When you lose the ball in or near the opponent's 18, this is the time to expend some fierce energy and burn some fuel because your team has a golden chance to win the ball back right away!

Did you notice how I didn't say *"the pressuring player"* has a golden chance? Nope, I said *"your team"* has a golden chance. And therein lies the rub. Oftentimes a player won't put her full effort into pressuring that opponent unless she feels she can get there in time to tackle the ball. Stay with me on this one, because this is a game-changer.

In this scenario, when the ball gets turned over and ends up on the foot of an opponent, her options are usually limited. The longer she has on the ball, the more viable her options become. With each passing fraction of a second, her chance of success grows. The worst possible outcome for you is if that opponent, who has just won the ball, connects a clean pass or clearance.

When you provide immediate pressure, your objective isn't necessarily to tackle the ball from her. Your objective is to make sure that opponent doesn't connect cleanly to a teammate. The work you do to pressure isn't necessarily for *you* to win the ball, but it may very well be for one of your teammates behind you to win the ball. That's why you hit the gas and burn some fuel in this situation, even if you are certain that you won't get there in time to put in a tackle. Your very simple objective is to put that opponent under enough pressure that she hits a ball that is less than ideal. Yes, tackling the ball directly might be the best possible outcome, but if that doesn't happen, your work can still produce a valuable consolation prize: possession of the ball for your team deep in the opponent's end of the field. Teams that do an effective job of creating sustained pressure around the penalty area produce a lot of goals.

When your team finds itself in the situation described above, I want you to remember the ten-yard rule: A player who is within ten yards of the ball should drop the hammer and go after it with everything she's got! She should burn some fuel and challenge that opponent to execute under maximum pressure, because oftentimes, the opponent won't be able to do it. In that area of the field, pressing players enjoy a wonderful freedom: They don't need to worry about principles of defense or team shape; instead they can just go psycho and hound the ball. This isn't the time to worry about advanced tactics; this is the time to buzz around like a lunatic and cause widespread panic. The pressing player might tackle the ball. She might deflect a pass. She might block a clearance. She might force an imperfect pass, or an unbalanced clearance that the opponent never gets off the ground. All types of wonderful things can happen when players expend energy at the right times.

Counter-pressing effectively requires the players, particularly the forwards, to be *selfless*. We're asking them to pressure with everything they've got, *even if the first player knows that she won't get there in time to tackle the ball,* just because it might give one of her teammates a better chance to win the ball. When your first layer pressures selflessly, the ball is often won by a teammate in the second or third layer. And just to be clear on this, oftentimes all we're really asking for is about three seconds of an all-out sprint. It might not seem worth it, but it is. It absolutely is worth it!

If you want to play a high-pressure style, selflessness is the single most important concept that the players must buy into, especially the forwards, because they're going to be the ones carrying the heaviest workload. They have to be willing to chase and chase and chase just so a teammate can end up winning the ball. That's not something every player can buy into, and a player who won't buy in will derail your team. To be successful at high pressure, your players have to be willing to work selflessly for the greater good.

20

The Pause

We've already touched on this topic a time or two, but it's important enough to warrant a chapter of its own.

Typically upon a change of possession, there's a brief pause from the team that has lost the ball as the players take a moment to grieve their misfortune. They are soon shaken back to reality by the realization that it's time to transition into their new job of putting pressure on the ball in an effort to win it back. Let me put it to you as simply as possible: That pause can kill you.

Any delay in getting pressure on the ball improves the opponent's chances of breaking our pressure. When we turn over the ball, we don't want players wallowing in a moment of self-pity, no matter how brief, before tending to their pressing duties. We want the transition from attacker to presser to be instantaneous! That's the genius of Barcelona's six-second rule: There's a very immediate deadline to correcting the mistake.

As you coach your team to press, look for those moments when possession has changed hands and stress immediate pressure. Emphasize the heck out of it! Loudly! Think of it like an experiment in electro-shock therapy. When your players delay in pressing, they get a shock. Before you know it, those delays get shorter and shorter until the pause disappears completely. When you have a team full of players dialed in to the immediate transition from attacker to presser, that's when you'll really see your press paying dividends.

Let's take this one step further and see if we can't start creating some psychics. You see, there's a difference between pressing after we lose possession and pressing when we're *about* to lose possession.

The ability to get immediate pressure on the ball after a turnover is a crucial element to successful pressure. We can coach our players to see the turnover and immediately press. That's an excellent quality, but let me give you one that's even better: the ability to transition into a pressing mode before the ball's been lost. In other words, recognizing that the ball is *about* to be lost.

Believe me, you will coach plenty of training exercises where it's painfully obvious that one team will be in the process of losing the ball, but its players will twiddle their thumbs until the ball officially changes hands. I've seen it happen more times than I can remember, and the only thing I can think to say is, "If you know you're gonna lose the ball, what the heck are you waiting for?" As a pressing coach, you are in a constant battle to transform recognition into action.

A player who sees that possession is about to change hands and immediately makes the transition is priceless. That's a player who eradicates the pause and imposes the greatest difficulty on the opponent. If you can coach even a few of your players to operate on that level, you're doing something very right.

The final section of this book is a collection of exercises to help you train a high-pressure team. A lot of these exercises hinge on the pressing team's ability to eliminate the pause from attacking to pressing. If you want your team to be successful at high pressure, this is where your bread is buttered.

21

Dogs

Okay, this is very similar to some of the previous material, but I think it's worth mentioning.

Oftentimes a player will chase the ball from one opponent to the next, as long as the ball is proceeding in something close to a singular direction. If I press a player who passes to his left, and then that player passes to his left, it's pretty likely that I'm going to chase both of those passes. As long as the ball is moving in a relatively straight direction, it's pretty easy to convince a player to chase.

We run into problems when the ball reverses directions. We're chasing a ball east when it suddenly turns and heads west. That requires us to slam on the brakes and then restart from scratch, and that's a lot more physically demanding and a lot less fun. And that's why a lot of players give up the chase when the ball reverses direction.

Understand that what I'm talking about here are those moments when the ball is deep in the opponent's territory and my player's willingness to chase will determine whether or not the opponent will survive the pressure. In those moments when the opponent connects a few quick passes in a small space, my player's willingness to pursue the ball in each and every direction is the most important factor in play. And so many players give up the hunt if they have to reverse direction, even if the finish line is just five yards away.

My dog Utley loves to chase tennis balls. If I throw a tennis ball in the living room, that dog's determination to get that ball is otherworldly. I'll throw the ball and Utley will chase it. Then, just before Utley catches up to it, the ball will bounce off the wall and head in the opposite direction. And Utley will chase it. Then the ball will hit a piece of furniture and change course again. And again, Utley will chase it. It doesn't matter how many times that ball changes direction, Utley's spirit never breaks. She just chases and chases and chases until she's got that ball. When the ball is pinging around near the opponent's goal, that's the same determination that you want to see in your players. To be effective at sustaining a press, your players have to be willing to do the hard chasing – the chasing that requires them to turn on a dime and immediately sprint again. And quite frankly, a lot of players just don't know that.

This willingness to change directions and chase isn't a skill, but it can be coached. It starts by letting your players know that their job isn't done just because the ball changed course. They have to be willing to give three more seconds of hard work for the greater good. When the moment calls for it, they have to be willing to chase like dogs.

22

The Payoff

There's a big psychological element to high pressure that you can't afford to ignore. You need forwards who are grinders. Your forwards are the tip of the spear. They are going to do more chasing than they might on some other teams, and their willingness to do that chasing is going to be heavily influenced by the rewards for their work. It's okay to ask your forwards to be selfless for the greater good. But if you're going to ask them to be selfless, you'd better darn well make sure the players behind them are busting their tails so that the hard work gets rewarded.

There is nothing more frustrating for a forward who has done the hard work of pressing at the right time than to see the opponent break pressure because a teammate in the second layer was late to the party. It won't take too many of those moments before that forward starts asking herself, "Why the heck am I doing all this running? What's the point?"

It takes a special kind of person to be a forward in a high pressure system. Those attacking personalities who will chase and tackle aren't run of the mill. A lot of forwards don't want to chase. They want their teammates to do the hard work and then drop the ball at their foot so they can go score. If you have even one forward whose attitude is, "You guys do the work and I'll score the goals," you'll never successfully implement high pressure. But if you are blessed with a few grinders who will do the grunt work up top, you have a priceless commodity that needs to be protected. You protect those players by making sure that their teammates have their backs. When the forwards cause an imperfect pass from the opponent, it is imperative that your team comes away with the ball. That's how the forwards see that their work is making a difference.

Counter-pressing isn't a solo act. It requires everyone in the vicinity of the ball to shift into a higher gear. Everyone has to share in the urgency to recover the ball. You can't have two workers and eight spectators. Everyone in a position to press the opponent needs to step up and physically impose themselves. It's that concerted team effort that turns their ball into your ball.

When your forwards embark on suicide missions for the greater good, they expect to see a payoff. Forwards who grind are the people you want on your team. Those are the people who put the success of the team ahead of their individual ambitions. They are the embodiment of teamwork. If you're going to ask them to be selfless, you'd better make darn sure that selflessness is reciprocated by the teammates behind them. That's the only way you'll sustain their willingness to keep chasing.

23

The Short Option

We've talked about staying connected. We've talked about asking our forwards to be selfless in their pursuit of the ball, and making sure that their teammates are fighting to reward that effort. If we are doing these things well, then ultimately we end up with a crowd around the ball, and that's what we want. We want to hunt in packs.

When we press up high, we are committing a lot of bodies to a relatively small area of the field. By condensing the space in which the opponent has to work, we are more likely to come away with the ball.

Let's say your right wing is pressing the opponent's left back. Your right back has moved up to deal with the left wing, who is offering a short passing option along the sideline. The question becomes, how tight should your right back stay to the left wing?

The right back's job is two-fold. First, she must clog the vertical seam to prevent a successful forward outlet pass. Her other job is to immediately press the left wing should the ball go to her.

In the next diagram, the right back is playing slightly off the left wing to protect the vertical seam into the target forward. She's conceding the shorter pass to protect against the bigger one. We're trying to force the opponent into a smaller and smaller space until there is nowhere left to go.

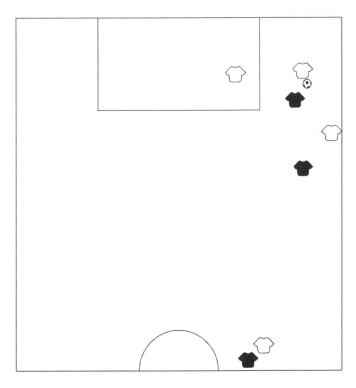

It is very important that the players in close support of the pressing team-mate – the right back in this case – read what's happening on the ball. It's not uncommon that the ball-carrier, in her attempts to escape pressure, will eliminate the vertical passing seam all by herself. If this happens, it frees up the right back to vacate that seam and commit to taking away the left wing as a short passing option.

For example, in the next diagram, the ball-carrier has turned her back to the field. This is a telltale cue to ratchet up your positional aggression. The vertical seam is no longer a viable option. Now the right back can really gamble with her positioning and try to eliminate the left wing as a passing option.

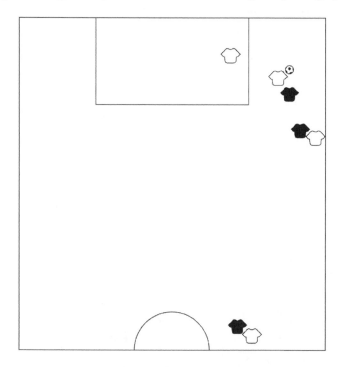

If you have the chance to eliminate the short option entirely, don't settle for being patient and defending after the pass is completed. Eliminate the passing seam entirely if the situation allows for it. When you take away that short option, the ball-carrier is stranded on an island and will often respond with a desperation attempt to clear the ball in some ill-advised direction. These moments of desperation often turn into exceptionally dangerous turnovers.

Additionally, if the area is tight enough, the supporting player can abandon her mark and double-team the ball. I wouldn't recommend this unless the supporting presser is within seven or eight yards of the ball and the ball-carrier is pinned near the boundaries. However, if the right back can pop off her mark and take an angle that eliminates that mark as a passing option, a double-team might be a great choice.

24

Funnels

As we've discussed, the first player in must make play predictable. This sets up your pressure funnel.

It's up to the coach to decide which way to funnel the opponent, and you have two choices: in or out. In their defensive half, many coaches prefer to funnel the opponent into the wide areas of the field. It's a perfectly logical choice because the wide areas are obviously away from the goal. However, some teams have been quite successful taking the opposite approach and funneling play to the inside. When the US upset Colombia in the 1994 World Cup, the Americans funneled the Colombian attack into the middle of the park and allowed center backs Marcelo Balboa and Alexi Lalas to showcase their abilities as ball-winners.

You get to make the same choice in the attacking end of the field, and your attacking funnel doesn't have to match your defensive one. But you really need to choose one side or the other. When your players step up to pressure the ball, they have to know where you want to steer the play.

Some coaches prefer to steer play wide. The benefit of this approach is that the sideline serves as an extra defender that severely limits the options of the player on the ball. The downside to this approach is that when you win the ball, you're winning it in the wide corridor and far from the goal.

The alternate approach is to funnel play into the center of the park. The upside is that if you win the ball, you're closer to the goal. The downside is that the players on the ball will have more passing options and will therefore be more likely to break your pressure.

Additionally, you can further customize this approach. For example, let's say the outside back is facing her own end-line when she's being pressured. You can use that as a cue to funnel her to the middle. If she is facing forward, that can be a cue to show her up the sideline. You could also swap these conditions.

Finally, you can customize this based on the side of the field. I've never seen a left-footed right back, but I've seen a large percentage of right-footed left backs. If you're playing a team with a right-footed left back and your objective is to take away each outside back's preferred foot, you could funnel the right back to the middle and the left back to the outside. As you can see, you've got options.

My default preference has been to funnel the opponent to the middle in our attacking half and to the outside in our defensive half, using the midfield stripe as the de facto line of demarcation. I've made adjustments for specific opponents, but that's where I like to start.

Let me also say that regardless of where you want to funnel the ball, there are times when a player needs to scrap the plan and improvise. If the opponent only has help to the outside, there aren't a lot of good reasons to show her that way. My point is that there are exceptions to the rule. In those instances, common sense needs to trump the plan.

However you decide to play it, the funnel is your trap. The objective is to force the ball into your funnel and then not let it out until you've won it. Doing this successfully requires a concerted team effort where each player understands and executes his role. The next page explains the roles of the various players in conjunction with the diagram. Keep in mind that your funnel must be fluid. You can't just set your funnel and expect one player to be the ball-winner. Forwards must be willing to double back to pressure the ball, and midfielders must be willing to charge forward if they have a chance to keep the opponent under pressure. The funnel only sets up the press; it's the players who actually execute it.

Interior Funnel – Roles

Let's diagram an interior funnel with our team set up in a 4-3-3, with two holding mids and one attacking mid.

You probably know that soccer has its own numbering system. Forgive me for not using it. In soccer's numbering system, the goalkeeper and defenders are assigned the lowest numbers and the attackers have the highest. For our purposes, I think it'll be easier if we assign the lower numbers to the players closest to the ball.

In this instance, because the ball-carrier is facing forward, the center forward plays slightly back from the pressing right wing. This allows him to help take away a potential, vertical passing seam and puts him in a position to double back if the ball goes into the funnel.

1. RW – Sets exterior edge of the funnel. Cuts off the outside and forces play into the middle. Goes after the ball. May double-team the ball.
2. CFWD – Eliminates LCB as passing option. Sets interior edge of the funnel. Will chase pass to goalkeeper or double back on a short pass into the funnel. May double-team the ball.
3. ACMF – First ball-winner in the funnel. Cannot allow opposing CMF to receive the ball and switch fields.
4. LW – Has to seal off the opponent from the opposite side of the field. Will challenge a pass into the RCB and possibly a pass into the goalkeeper. If the ball is played over the top to the RB, must turn and angle into a retreating run.
5. RB – Cuts out at least some of a vertical passing seam while staying near enough to pressure opposing LW.
6. DCMF – Second ball-winner in the funnel.
7. DCMF – Playing centerfield. Responsible for any ball that squirts through the funnel. Helping to screen against the center forward.
8. RCB – Marks CFWD
9. LCB – Provides deep cover for any ball over the top
10. LB – Marks RW

Interior Funnel – Ball-Carrier Facing Forward

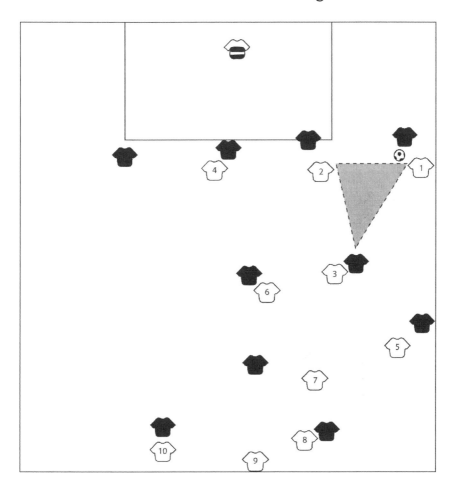

Interior Funnel — Ball-Carrier Facing End-Line

In this instance, because the ball-carrier is facing his own end-line, the center forward doesn't need to worry about cutting out a vertical seam. Now he plays slightly ahead of the pressing right wing to cut off an attempted pass to the goalkeeper and has more freedom to move toward the ball for a double-team.

The left wing can creep a little more centrally to look for a loose ball or an errant pass. The right back doesn't need to remain goal-side of the left-wing. It's important to remember that these positions aren't static. Each player on the pressuring team must read and react to the changes occurring on the ball.

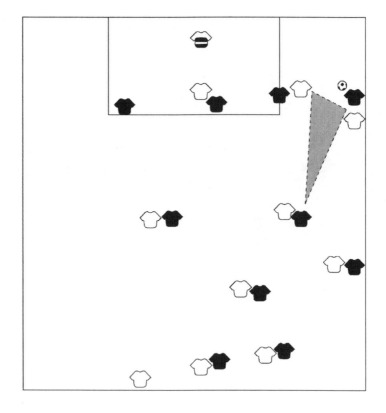

25

Screening

I went back and forth about including this topic in *Shutout Pizza*, but since that book focuses specifically on the back four, I opted not to address it. However, screening is a vital part of a well-organized team defense, regardless of your system of pressure. Here's the good news: Very few coaches actually understand it, let alone teach it. If you can make it a part of your defensive scheme, you'll have at least one very clear-cut advantage over most of your opponents.

Screening is placing a player between the ball and a target in advance of the ball – typically an opposing forward. The screening player isn't concerned with marking an opponent, but rather clogging the seam from the ball-carrier to a forward target. If you've ever heard about a player whose role is to 'protect the back four,' that is a reference to screening.

I reckon that if you thought about it, you could probably conjure up situations where almost any player could serve as a screen, but by and large the role of a screen will fall to a midfielder, and in particular, a defensive (or holding) midfielder. This is a player whose positioning will often be dictated by the ball and not by marking any specific opponent.

The value of screening is that it takes away one of the ball-carrier's best options – a longer pass that penetrates beyond our second layer. Translating that into our high-pressure set-up, a well-executed screen will often force the ball-carrier to spend more time with the ball at his feet trying to figure out his next move. Any delay we cause him gives us more time to close down and make a challenge on the ball. Our screen may also force the ball-carrier to play a much shorter pass, helping us to contain the opponent to a small space and allowing us to exert more pressure on the ball. Any way you slice it, a proper screen eliminates one of the opponent's best escape hatches.

Screen 1

In this diagram, the left back has evaded our first pressuring player. An opposing forward is checking off the right center back. A second, weak-side attacker has moved laterally into the center back's zone, which prevents the center back from going with the checking forward. That leaves the first forward in a sort of cushion between our defensive and midfield layers. There is a clear seam between the ball and the target forward.

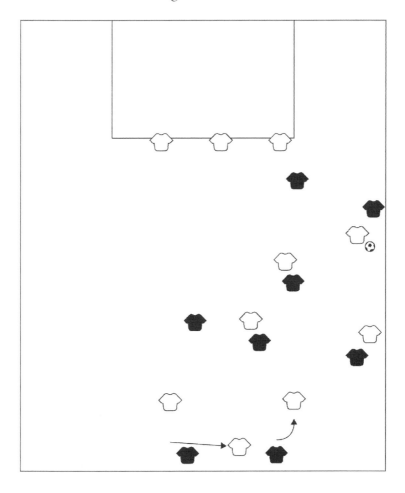

As you see in the diagram, there is no one available to mark the checking forward. The only solution is to cut out the seam between that forward and the ball. We do that by maneuvering our defensive center-mid into the seam.

It's pretty easy to understand, but it can be a lot more difficult to execute. The problem for our holding midfielder is that he doesn't have eyes in the back of his head. To be an effective screener, you have to be constantly taking looks behind you to locate the target. But even then, there's nothing stopping the target from making counter-moves to our midfielder's positioning. Our holding midfielder can't simply watch the target; he must also watch the ball. And when he watches the ball, there's an excellent chance that the forward will do some type of vanishing act.

A smart and vocal center back can greatly aid the efforts of our holding midfielder by merely shouting, "Step right," or "Step left!" In the previous diagram, the seam into the target was to the right of our holding midfielder, but not by much. In the next diagram, look what happens if the center back steers our holding mid a few steps to the right. Now our holding mid has cut out the seam entirely.

Screen 2

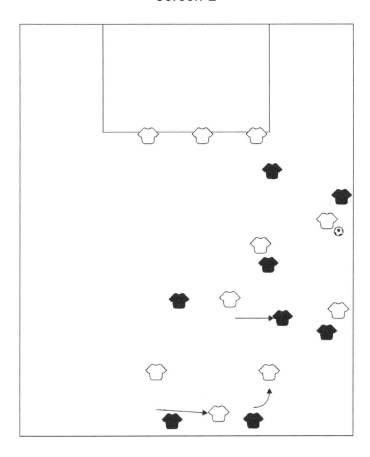

It's a simple solution if you have a center back with a soccer IQ high enough to understand seams and recognize the opportunity to clog the seam into the forward, and a holding mid who is willing to listen to his center back. For this to work, the center back has to virtually operate the holding mid via remote control. When the center back says, "One step right," the holding mid must immediately adjust to the instructions.

It's also imperative that our holding mid doesn't vacate that seam in order to chase/mark an opponent who is leaving that seam. For example, in the next diagram, the holding mid is marking the opponent's attacking mid and together they are clogging the seam into the forward. The opponent moves centrally, hoping to drag the holding mid out of the seam to clear a path for the ball. If the holding mid takes the bait, the seam opens up and the ball is quickly advanced to the target. It takes a bit of nerve to stand in a no-man's land occupying a space when everyone else seems so busy. That's why it's important for all of our players to understand the principles of big-picture defending. Players who are determined to man-mark opponents are easy to manipulate. But if they understand the value of positioning, they'll know when the best thing they can do is hold their ground.

One last note about screening: Oftentimes the screening player won't intercept the pass, simply because the pass into the target never materializes. The ball-carrier sees the screen and realizes the pass won't get there, so he starts looking for a different solution. In that sense, the screener serves as a deterrent. However, plenty of times the ball-carrier will try to squeeze the ball past our screen anyway, and our screener will end up with the ball. Now, that said, our screening player can also try baiting the pass into the target. Instead of standing directly along the line between the ball and the target, the screener can position himself a yard or so off that line and invite the pass. If the ball-carrier takes the bait, the screener can jump the ball as it is coming off the opponent's foot and intercept the pass. This is a pretty savvy maneuver, but it's really not that difficult for a smart player to execute.

Screen 3

As the opponent's attacking center mid curls out of the seam, our holding mid maintains his position to prevent a path from the ball into a target forward.

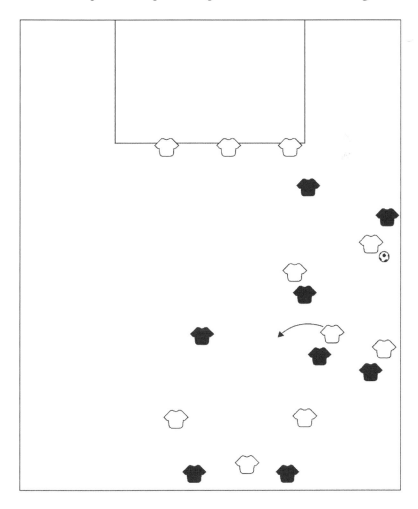

26

Hide and Seek

When the opponent has the ball, regardless of where we set our restraining line, there are passes we want to eliminate, and there are passes we want to bait. The value of eliminating a certain pass is that the pass never materializes and thus can't hurt us. But when we eliminate a passing option, that potential pass can't help us either. In other words, we won't have the opportunity to pick it off and win possession. This is a game of cat and mouse and knowing how to play it well is extremely beneficial.

To eliminate a pass, our player just needs to stay tight to the potential target to deter the pass. To bait a pass, our player needs to stay a little looser to the target. The idea is to give the pass an illusion of attractiveness. When the ball-carrier takes the bait, our player pounces to intercept the ball.

If your system depends heavily on your wings pressing the opposing outside backs, one of the most important players will be your center forward, or whoever takes up that central position. She sets up the interior edge of your funnel. She is also often the one who can convert pressure into turnovers. I want to specifically address a situation where the opposing outside back is moving toward her own end-line and your center forward sets up the funnel's interior edge.

As the winger begins to press, the center forward is basically playing a non-committal centerfield. She has to evaluate when to move forward toward the goalkeeper, when to stay put to deny a lateral escape, and when to drop off to protect against a potential vertical pass. To do this job effectively, she has to read the pressure on the ball, read the ball-carrier's body language and understand the options available to the ball-carrier.

If the ball-carrier puts the ball between her body and the sideline, the center forward should put on the brakes and prepare for the ball to be played forward up the line. If the ball-carrier puts the ball either directly between herself and the end-line, or between herself and the middle of the field, the center forward should begin to move forward in anticipation of a pass to the center back or the goalkeeper.

Here's the thing... this isn't a one-move show. As the player on the ball twists and turns, the center forward needs to make the corresponding adjustments. She may need to take a couple of steps forward, a step back, then a few more forward. Her job is reactive and hinges on her ability to anticipate what the ball-carrier will do with the ball.

One of the most effective adjustments the center forward can make in this process is to play a little hide-and-seek from the opponent on the ball. With the outside back facing her own end-line, the goalkeeper becomes a likely target for the next pass. In this situation, there is no better outcome than having your center forward intercept that pass. Where most players get this wrong is that they leave too soon in anticipation of that pass. They'll give away their intentions and slide too close to that passing seam. As soon as the ball-carrier notices the forward's intentions, the last place she's ever going to play that ball is to the goalkeeper. That's not what we want. We don't want to deter that pass; we want to bait it!

The solution is for the center forward to keep herself out of the ball-carrier's field of vision while reading the ball-carrier's body language. The moment the ball-carrier's body language indicates a pass to the goalkeeper, that's the center forward's cue to get on her horse and burst into that seam and pick off the pass.

Is this easy? No way. You need a pretty good soccer IQ to recognize the cue to get moving, and even then there's no guarantee you'll get there in time. By playing hide-and-seek, you're leaving yourself more ground to cover. But on the flipside, the payoff is absolutely worth it, because if you can get onto just one of those back-passes, you can change the game. If you happen to be playing an opponent that liberally back-passes to its keeper, this is a discussion worth having with your forwards.

27

The Weak-Side Winger

Let's stay with our three-front and say our right wing is pressing the opponent's left back. Our left wing's primary job is to not allow the ball to escape to the right back, so he's going to sit in the middle as a spy and react to the ball. We want him to contest any ball that's intended for the right-center back. If the ball reaches the right-center back, our left wing must, at the very least, force play back into the funnel. He has to seal off the opponent. In a press, that's a fundamental role for the weak-side winger: Cut off the weak side of the field.

There's another really important thing to know about this player, and chances are that your players won't know this unless you tell them: The weak-side attacker is often the most dangerous attacker once possession changes hands. He's like a secret agent behind enemy lines. He's often positioned directly in front of the goal and he's also the player that the defenders are most likely to lose track of.

The ball is like a magnet and it's going to pull people toward it from both teams. If we can turn over the opponent on the crowded side of the field, there's an excellent chance that our weak-side winger is in a position to capitalize. All we have to do is figure out how to immediately get him the ball. I can't tell you exactly how to do that, but I know it starts with that weak-side player understanding his role and his opportunity.

I'm telling you this so you can use this information to turn turnovers into chances. Even though he may be physically away from the play, the weak-side winger needs to stay switched on to the possibilities once a turnover has materialized. He needs to be alert and attentive to gaps in the defense. And he needs to be ready to get moving.

The biggest value to pressing up high is that you can win the ball close to the opponent's goal. You can create chances quickly without crafting your way through an organized defense. If you're going to win the ball up high, you can't forget about the second part of the equation – the attacking part.

When you do pressing exercises in training, let your players know the value of the weak-side winger. He is often the fastest way to turn defensive pressure into attacking danger. When your players force a turnover, the weak-side winger doesn't have to be their first pass, but if conditions allow for it, he should certainly warrant consideration as their first look.

Weak-Side Winger

In this diagram, as the first two attackers set the top edge of the funnel, the weak-side winger shifts into the center of the park to prevent the opponent from switching fields.

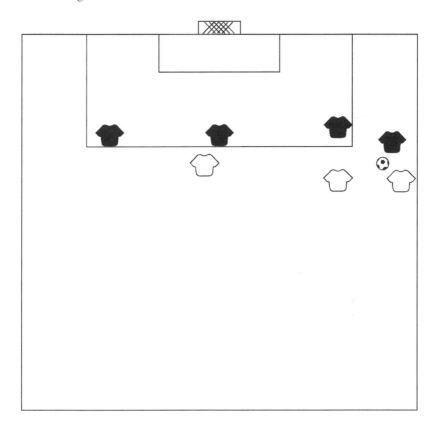

28

The Ball-Winners

If you set up an interior funnel, the players in that funnel had better be aggressive ball-winners. If you set up an exterior funnel, the sideline will solve some of your problems. That's not the case when you force the ball into the middle of the field and likely into the opponent's most skilled players.

The back half of your funnel will typically be occupied by central midfielders. If those players aren't much for tackling, you're going to have problems. When the ball goes into the funnel, it can't come out. It needs to be won. Winning it requires aggressive ball-winners with a first-to-the-ball attitude, who can read the play and jump the pass. The players who comprise your funnel have to understand the urgency of their roles. They have to know that everyone else is setting the table for them and that they need to step up and deliver.

One of the most common mistakes these players will make is to hold their position goal-side of an opponent who offers support inside the funnel. By staying goal-side, you allow the opponent to keep his body between you and the ball, making it difficult to put an actual challenge in on the ball. If the opponent is comfortable playing with pressure on his back – and most good players are – it

94

becomes exceptionally difficult to dislodge him from the ball. So the easiest solution is to prevent that opponent from being first to the ball, but you can't do that if your starting position is goal-side.

As it becomes clear that the ball will be played in to the funnel, your players in that funnel have to take up more aggressive positions against opponents checking back to receive the ball. If at all possible, your players should try to move from behind their marks to beside their marks as the ball begins its journey. We want our players to have an opportunity to make a play on the ball, and that's not going to happen if we allow the opponent to separate them from the ball. When the ball arrives, we ideally want to be the first one to it, even if by just a toe's length. If we can't be first, we want to put the opposing player under so much duress that it becomes extremely difficult to receive the ball cleanly. To be honest, in this situation I would prefer my players to be overly aggressive than not aggressive enough. In other words, I would prefer to be whistled for a foul than to have the opponent come cleanly out of the funnel and switch fields. Obviously neither of those outcomes is ideal. Ideally we want our funnel to apply enough pressure to force a turnover. I'm just saying I'd rather our effort be too strong than too weak.

29

4-4-2 Shift

If you play in a 4-4-2, oftentimes the responsibility for pressing the opponent's outside backs will fall upon your wide midfielders. Sometimes a striker will get there in time to press and set up your funnel, but there will also be plenty of occasions when there is too much ground for the forward to cover. In these instances we can implement a shift of our back four that frees up the outside midfielder. This is especially important if our opponent is playing with wide midfielders.

So let's say we're playing a 4-4-2 against another 4-4-2. Our outside midfielders will spend a good bit of their day marking and dueling with the opponent's outside midfielders. But if our right midfielder steps up to press the opponent's left back, the opponent's left midfielder is left unmarked. The shift is how we solve this problem.

As our right midfielder moves forward, our right back steps up to the opposing left midfielder and all the other defenders move one slot to the right. Our right-center back slides out to become a right back; our left-center back becomes our right-center back; and our left back becomes our left-center back, and as long as our press holds, we play without a left back.

This shift is pretty simple to execute as long as the players recognize the cues and effectively communicate. However, if the right back is late to the party, it can become one of those situations we discussed where the opponent tic-tac-toes its way through our defensive block. Typically, if the first player is a second late, everyone supporting her is at least a second late and that's where we can run into big problems.

The right back has to stay tuned into what her outside midfielder is doing. As a matter of fact, I prefer that the outside back actually dictates the press to her midfielder. As the ball begins working its way to their side of the field, the outside back can start communicating to the midfielder, saying something like, "Pat, get ready... get ready.... Go, go, go!" That type of communication assures us that the players are on the same page and it allows the midfielder to press with confidence.

4-4-2 Shift

In this diagram, the right midfielder steps up to press the opponent's left back, while the right back moves forward to press the left midfielder. The other defenders slide one slot to their right. Once the shift is complete, the pressing team is playing without a left back.

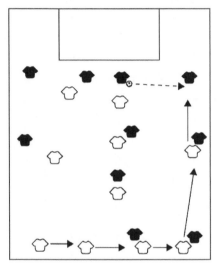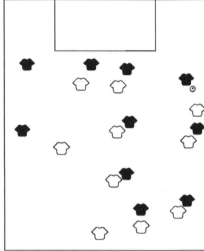

30

Pressing from a 3-5-2

As with a 4-4-2, playing from a 3-5-2 leaves you with only two players in your highest layer. Therefore we must figure out how to incorporate our other layers if we are going to effectively high press the opponent.

As I said at the outset, there are too many variables in play to explain every permutation of every situation that could potentially occur during a soccer match, so I'm just going to give you some broad strokes as well as some considerations that your players must factor into their decision-making process.

For simplicity sake, let's say that we're playing our middle three in a triangle and not flat. Our midfield triangle has one attacking midfielder and two holding midfielders. In coaching parlance, we're playing two low and one high in the middle. Let's put the opponent in a 4-4-2, and let's set our restraining line thirty-five yards from the opposing goal. The goalkeeper has the ball in hand at the center of the eighteen. Both teams are centrally balanced.

If the opponent splits its center backs to the corners of the eighteen and pushes its outside backs up the field, our strong-side center forward has to be the one to press on the ball. The other center forward will shift toward the ball and be responsible for any pass into the goalkeeper or weak-side center back. Everyone behind them will have to match up. This set-up leaves us matched up man to man in every spot. We have the option of pulling our weak-side winger into the back four to free up the strong-side outside back. Another option is to rotate a holding mid into a center back slot with the same intention of freeing up the strong-side outside back. These are the decisions you get to make.

If the opponent doesn't split the center backs and the goalkeeper distributes to the left back, we have to decide which of our players will step up to pressure the ball. Again, if the strong-side center forward is close enough to do the job, then that is our best option. In this example, it is most likely that, due to the distance covered and the angle of approach, our forward will be unable to set up an interior funnel, in which case we'll have to rely on an exterior funnel. Our other forward will shift toward the ball-side of the field, and our right-side midfielder will stay home to match up against the opposing left midfielder. Our own left midfielder will squeeze centrally to shore up our numbers in the center of the park. Our attacking center mid will step up as a slightly withdrawn forward to deal with the strong-side center back. His job isn't necessarily to take away the center back as an option, but rather to bait a pass into that player that can be immediately pressured. If he does step up to the center back, one of our holding mids must step to the opposing holding mid (Diagram A). That's one way to play it.

3-5-2 Press

In this example, the strong-side forward steps to pressure and set up an exterior funnel.

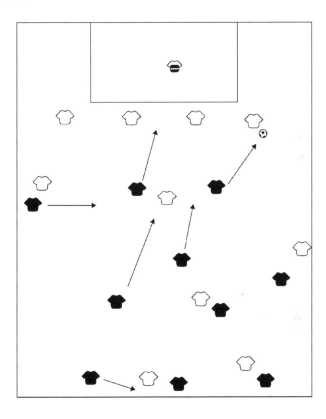

A second option is to push our right midfielder onto the ball. Moving our right midfielder onto the ball obviously requires him to abandon the opponent's left midfielder and that's a risky endeavor. Because we are playing in a three-back system, it may not be realistic to expect our right back to roll up to the opposing left midfielder; there's likely too much ground to cover. That leaves our right midfielder on the wrong end of a 2v1.

I'm not going to take a deep dive into this approach because I'm not a fan of it, and I'm certainly not recommending it. I only offer it because I've seen it used. I don't mind the right midfielder stepping up a bit to deter the left back from chewing up ground on the dribble, but I don't like the idea of him committing all out unless he is absolutely certain to win the ball due to some technical failure on the opposition's behalf. Otherwise, it's my belief that he is better served by staying home.

A third option is to push a center mid onto the ball. This is a pretty standard fallback approach if our forwards are caught too far away to do the job themselves, which is a reality that will occur from time to time, even if we're playing in a 4-3-3. For example, let's say our forwards have shifted toward our attacking left side and the opponent quickly switches the ball to the outside back on the far side of the field. At that point the opponent has broken pressure and it's up to the nearest member of our midfield three to slide out and confront the ball. As our team is temporarily unbalanced, it's not the pressuring midfielder's job to go and win the ball, but rather to absorb the attack and slow the opponent's progress as his teammates retreat to form up the defensive block.

Sending a center mid to pressure the ball allows our right midfielder to stay home and match up against the opposing left midfielder. If we're going to play it this way, then we will likely need a rotation amongst the other center midfielders. If, for example, our holding mid moves out to pressure, the other holding mid must immediately slide over to match up with the opposing attacking mid.

As you can see, there are plenty of variations, and variations within the variations, and variations within those variations. And that's not because we're playing from a 3-5-2. That's just soccer. It's a fluid game and the picture is constantly in flux. There are a million and one if-then contingencies, and as coaches we spend our lives trying to bring some order to the chaos. Remember, it's not the system that dictates success or failure; it's the manner in which we implement that system. Regardless of the system we select, the important thing is that our players understand their roles and understand their list of priorities at any given moment. They need to know how to adapt to an unpredictable environment that demands constant adaptations.

3-5-2 Press – Pressure Broken

In this example, a holding center mid slides out to confront the ball-carrier once the opponent has broken pressure.

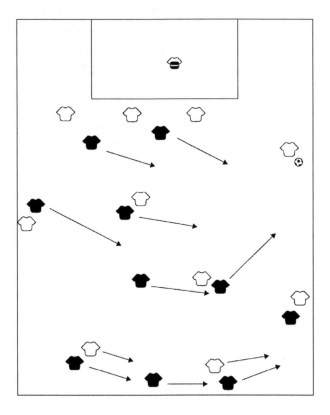

31

The Defensive Line

M ost of this book focuses on how to defend as a team in the opponent's half of the field. This chapter is a little different because we'll be talking mainly about situations where the opponent has the ball and our defenders have retreated into our half of the field. And the material we're about to cover isn't exclusive to a high pressure style of play. It's just about good soccer sense. I urge you to digest this information and absorb it into your coaching philosophy. It can make a radical difference in your team's ability to keep the opponent under pressure by forcing them to play on a crowded field.

Just to make sure we're all speaking the same language here, a defensive line refers to the positioning of our line of defenders. It is the horizontal line our deepest backs will occupy, typically somewhere between our own eighteen and the midfield stripe, when the opponent has the ball. Basically it's where our defenders set up shop.

We could, in theory, hold our line lower than the eighteen, but that would turn our goal into a shooting gallery. At some point we have to stop giving ground, and that point is usually higher than the eighteen. We could, also theoretically, hold our line higher than the midfield stripe, but as the midfield stripe sets the offside line, that would be rather suicidal. That's not to say our defenders won't ever collapse into our eighteen or push beyond the midfield stripe, because often times they will. The defensive line generally refers to where our defenders will stop their retreat, at least temporarily, as the opponent advances the ball. This line is not stationary. It will advance as the ball travels towards the opposing goal, and it will drop as the opponent advances the ball toward our goal.

Let's see if I can simplify this a little bit. The opposition's center back has the ball on his half of midfield, unpressured, right on the center circle. So we set our defensive line thirty-five yards from the ball. This is the distance that we feel we can adequately deal with any attempt to play a long ball over the top of our defenders. At this distance we feel our defenders will either have a chance to head away a long-ball attempt or, if the ball is hit too far for our defenders to make a play on it, our goalkeeper will be able to mop things up.

Setting your line is an important, and often overlooked, part of tactical soccer. How far do we step up? And how far do we retreat? Set your line too low and the opposition can stretch you out; set it too high and you risk being victimized by balls in behind your defense. We must be able to set a proper line and recognize cues that signal our line to step forward or retreat.

So, exactly how deep should we set our line? Well, that's a matter of philosophy, but the previous example gives you a pretty reasonable standard. Most coaches want their line pushed as far forward as possible without exposing themselves to a ball that gets in behind their defense. But that's most coaches, and definitely not all of them. Some coaches prefer their defenders to play a high line.

If our team is known to 'hold a high line,' it means that when the opponent is in possession, our line of defenders is higher up the field than you might expect, and that the line of defenders is reluctant to drop off. Instead of retreating in response to a visual cue, our defenders might hold their ground to let the opposing attackers run offside. Teams that hold a high line leave a lot of space between the defenders and the goalkeeper and only drop when absolutely necessary. They tend to invite the opponent to play over the top of them, which is why it's a really good idea to have fast defenders and an exceptionally mobile and aggressive goalkeeper if you plan to play a high line.

A high line is a live-by-the-sword proposition to be sure. The upside is that it pushes opposing forwards back toward their midfield. This, in turn, keeps the field congested, which limits the amount of space and time the opponent has on the ball. A high line is also likely to induce more offside calls, which can make it frustrating to play against.

The downside to the high line is *all that space* between the defenders and the goalkeeper. One well-timed pass into a well-timed run and the opponent is behind you. Teams that hold a high line are daring opponents to play behind them, particularly with balls over the top. They are also banking on the players ahead of their defenders – the midfielders and forwards – to keep the opponent under constant pressure to prevent delivery of that killer ball.

Where you set your line is a matter of preference. However, having a high line or a low line is a secondary consideration to what really matters – having a mobile line. A mobile line is one that stays active, dropping off when it needs to and sprinting forward when it can.

If we're going to be a high-pressure team, we want our defenders moving aggressively forward when the opportunity presents itself. We want the opponent to play on a crowded field. If we're going to press well, we can't allow the opponent to stretch out our layers. We need to squeeze the field from back to front. In other words, we can't let the opposing forwards set our line.

Our backs need to dictate our line. When the opponent is in possession, our defenders need to set a high line whenever possible to keep everyone packed

into a relatively tight space. If our backs drop off just because the opposing forwards start walking toward our goal, the gaps between our layers will expand,
our team shape will get stretched and we'll be vulnerable in those gaps. By that
same token, if the ball moves towards the opponent's goal and our defenders
don't advance, the result is the same: We get stretched.

There are going to be a multitude of occasions when our line needs to drop,
even if it just pushed forward just a second earlier. When and how far our line
drops is a matter of philosophy. I think there are certain cues that should signal
our defenders to immediately retreat. For example, if a player on the opposing
team has possession and is in a good position to play a long ball forward, I want
my defenders dropping to prevent the ball over the top.

Other coaches would look at this same cue and prefer that their line holds
right where it's at. If your team holds a high line against an opponent that has
track-star attackers, you've got more nerve than me. For starters, you're putting
an awful lot of faith in the assistant referee's ability to judge offside. And that's
just for the plays that are actually offside. Like I said, one well-time pass into a
well-timed run and your high line suddenly has some big problems.

In spite of the previous paragraph, I'm not a total coward. I firmly believe
that our line of defenders should aggressively push forward whenever prudent.
Yes, there are certainly cues that should signal those players to drop off, but
until one of those cues reveals itself, our backs need to maintain a relatively high
line. That high line decreases the gap between our defenders and our midfielders, and between our midfielders and forwards. If our defenders retreat because
they recognize that a long ball might be coming, but then that long ball never
materializes, those defenders must immediately move forward again to reclaim
that territory and squeeze the field from back to front. If we're going to effectively high press, our defensive line has to be mobile and our defenders need to
exploit opportunities to steal ground. How much ground we're willing to steal
and how long we're willing to hold that ground, well, that will be dictated by
any number of factors and it can vary from one opponent to the next.

A failure to steal ground from the back is one of the most common tactical failures I've seen in American youth soccer. Sure, a team that's not in possession will drift forward if the ball moves in that same direction, but precious few teams step forward with an urgency of purpose. I think that's because most players and coaches don't understand the value of stealing ground from the back. Players only move forward because the ball moved forward and players just gravitate to the ball. But if the players understood that by quickly stepping forward they could run the opposition's attackers back into their midfielders and in turn, burden the opponent with a congested field, then they would understand the higher purpose of stepping and react more quickly and effectively.

I'll give you an example that happens all the time. Let's say an opposing center mid has the ball at the bottom edge of the center circle, on our half of midfield, where he is confronted by our center forward. There's a pretty reasonable likelihood that our defensive line would be just out in front of our 18, maybe two or three steps in front of the 'D.' Now that midfielder turns around and plays a negative ball to his center back, who is standing on midfield. If our center forward chases that pass, but our defensive line stays where it's at, our defensive block just got stretched out to the tune of ten yards. However, if our defenders immediately stole ten yards when the ball went negative, we could run the opposing forwards back on top of their midfielders and crowd the field. (Incidentally, if our defenders are going to sprint to steal back those ten yards, our midfielders and forwards need to do the same thing on the same cue.)

Just to be clear, the ball doesn't have to be going toward the far end of the field for us to steal ground. We can also steal ground on square passes, particularly longer ones played between opposing defenders. We may have to immediately give that ground back, especially if the receiver of the pass can play a long ball forward, but we temporarily forced the opposing attackers away from our goal and crowded the field. If the player who received the pass can't play forward, we may not have to give that ground back at all.

I love watching a group of defenders that understands the value of stealing ground, because so much is happening off the ball. Their line is very active because those defenders are constantly adjusting. They are constantly giving ground and then stealing it back. At times it looks like they're hosting their own micro track meet. If they can steal five yards, they steal those yards immediately. Even when the ball is thirty or forty yards away, they are fighting for every inch of territory and the opposing forwards are constantly challenged to get back to an onside position. Playing against a defensive line that actively steals ground will suck the fun right out of a forward's day. For starters, that forward has to do a lot more running than he's accustomed to, and a good bit of that running is away from the goal he wants to attack. It can be an irritating, frustrating and exhausting experience.

The ability to squeeze the field from back to front is what keeps our players – not just our defenders, all our players – in position to quickly put pressure on the ball. It's what forces the opponent to execute with a minimum of time and space. Squeezing the field starts with where we set our line and how quickly we recognize and react to cues.

Your opponent's personnel and style of play are important factors to consider when deciding how you'll set your line. An opponent that is good at banging balls over the top might inspire you to set your line a little bit lower. An opponent that refuses to play over the top may be an invitation for you to hold your line higher. Regardless of where you set your line, you need to squeeze the field from back to front whenever prudent if you want to exert maximum pressure on the opponent.

32

Position First

"Get your position, then you rest! Get your position, then you rest!" That sentence is burned deep into my soul. I can still hear my college coaches shouting it over and over and over again like some sort of Gregorian chant. We were a high pressure team, and this was one of our tenets. I specifically recall hearing this loop when we were playing the Sheffield Wednesday exercise, which will be provided in the next section.

Get your position, then you rest. It refers to the order of priorities when a dead ball occurs. When the run of play is interrupted, either by the referee's whistle or the ball crossing the boundary or the goalkeeper grabbing the ball, a player's natural reaction is to take a rest – physically and mentally – before refocusing on the task at hand. As coaches, our job is to realign the priorities of our players.

One of the simplest ways to break pressure is to get out before the pressure is organized. A team that takes quick restarts can slip our noose before we even tie the knot. We can't let that happen.

The easiest way to prevent this little vanishing act is to get organized before the ball is restarted. That takes a concerted mental and physical effort from players who are often winded and happy to have a break in the action. We have to condition our players to stay switched on and to postpone resting until the time is right. That's why my college coaches fed us a steady diet of 'Get your position, then you rest!' And that's why I have, in turn, fed it to twenty-some years of my own players.

When the opponent has been gifted a restart, there has to be an urgency to making sure our own house is in order. We have to be in a position to press the instant play is restarted. We can't provide our opponent with an escape hatch just because we need a breather. We've got to take care of first things first, and that means taking up the best possible position so we are able to immediately reactivate our press. Organizing quickly will, among other things, deter the quick restart. It will force the opponent to pause and evaluate its options. We take our rest during that pause.

Putting organization ahead of rest isn't exclusive to high pressure defending; it's an all-around good soccer policy. But it is critical for a team that wants to sustain pressure in the attacking third of the field. If you're going to play all out high pressure, you need players who stay on high alert because there's an urgency to applying that pressure. When you get the opponents penned deep in their own end, the objective is to keep them there. You can't have players switching off just because the goalkeeper snagged a cross or the ball rolled over the end-line. If you do, your pressure will spring a lot of leaks.

There's nothing wrong with taking a rest. Smart players are always looking for opportunities to rest. Resting is a good thing – as long as we're resting at the right times. And when it comes to an opponent's restart, the time to rest is after we've gotten our own team organized. So we position first. Then we rest.

33

Communication

During the Civil War, Confederate soldiers were known to preface a charge with a raucous battle cry that came to be known as the Rebel Yell. The yell served several purposes. It was a signal across the troops that the charge was commencing; it was a coping mechanism to help the Rebels summons the courage to join that charge; and it was an instrument of intimidation against the Union troops. In other words, it was the Rebels' way of saying, "Make 'em hate it!" Union soldiers reported that the Rebel Yell could induce paralyzing fear amongst their troops before they could even see the enemy.

Communication on a soccer field works the same way. It is an instrument of both information and intimidation.

High pressure is a blunt force ballet. It combines tireless effort with precision choreography. Everyone has an important role to play and the ability to communicate information is a critical component to keeping your team organized and its shape intact. That doesn't change if you're playing high pressure or low pressure or something in between. It doesn't change if you have possession of the ball or your opponent does. Any way you slice it, information is power.

As we've discussed at length, a key to successful high pressure is keeping your layers connected, back to front and side to side. That won't happen without open and generous lines of communication. If you fail to communicate, you'll end up with a lot of holes in your blanket. But if you've got an organized team that will press as one connected unit, communication becomes much more than just the give and take of information. If done properly, it becomes your Rebel Yell.

There is something very unsettling when you are chasing a ball back toward your own goal and you hear the opponent announcing his plans. First you hear a chorus of, "Press, press, press!," and you know that someone will soon be breathing down your neck. Then you hear, "Force him inside," and you know that you're headed straight into a trap. As your operating space shrinks, the voices are getting louder and louder until the only voices you hear are coming from your opponents. You're stranded on your own little island and there doesn't appear to be any help on the way. So what do you do? You begin to second guess yourself. A moment later you start to panic. Nothing good happens after that.

When used properly, communication is intimidation. I've seen teams wholly undone by it. I've seen twenty-year-old men crumble beneath it. When you're the player on the ball and you hear the opponent's level of communication crest, you know they are about to spring their trap. In that moment, it's easy to forget that you're a soccer player and to start thinking of yourself as the prey. And then you and every teammate near you starts thinking the same thing: *Get this freaking ball away from me!* That's how a team unravels.

When the time comes to spring your trap, you want players loudly and enthusiastically sharing that information. It will cause their adrenalin to surge while simultaneously inducing widespread panic in the opponent.

When you press, don't keep it a secret. You're taking the battle to the opponent. You're choosing your moment to make 'em hate it. Don't do it quietly. Use your voice to induce maximum mayhem. Let it be your Rebel Yell.

34

Work Rate

Once upon a time, there used to be an annual college soccer game between the Division I national champion and the NAIA national champion. I had the chance to attend one of these games in the spring of 1995. The NAIA's West Virginia Wesleyan was squaring off with Bruce Arena's dynasty from the University of Virginia. A few months earlier UVA had just claimed its fourth consecutive national title. The Virginia program was the most dominant program in the history of men's college soccer and had produced the United States' top national team talent. Names like Harkes, Reyna and Meola had all been Cavaliers. Seven thousand soccer fans attended that afternoon in Atlanta, and most of them had come out to watch Virginia put on a show. It was clearly a pro-UVA crowd. Few in attendance had ever heard of the NAIA, and fewer still had heard of West Virginia Wesleyan.

With less than ten minutes remaining, and the score tied 1-1, a forward nicked the ball from the center back at the top of the eighteen and looked poised to score. The panicked defender swatted out the attacker's legs and the forward crashed to the ground. It was clearly a foul. The entire stadium erupted in anticipation of the referee's whistle for a penalty kick. But the whistle never came. The one man in the stadium who didn't see the foul was the referee.

And then it happened.

Thousands of soccer fans began whistling their displeasure.

I had never heard American soccer fans whistling in discontent before that day. Europeans have a longstanding tradition of whistling their disapproval, but not Americans. Americans boo. At least we did until that day. But the whistling was only the second-most surprising aspect of that moment. You see, it was a forward from West Virginia Wesleyan who had been fouled, and a penalty kick probably would have won the day for the NAIA. Instead the game ended in a 1-1 tie.

Have you seen Rocky IV? It's the one where Rocky beats the Russian. Their final fight is in Moscow, and in the beginning the entire arena is forcefully behind their hometown boy. But as the fight wears on, Rocky begins to win over the crowd and, by the end, thousands of Russians are chanting, "Rah-key! Rah-key!" Pretty cheesy, right? Well, this soccer game was a heckuva lot like that movie. The crowd had abandoned its allegiance to UVA. The West Virginia Wesleyan Bobcats had systematically won the hearts and minds of that stadium full of soccer fans, and they did it with sound soccer, a big heart, and an awful lot of good ol' fashioned hard work.

West Virginia Wesleyan pressured the snot out of UVA that day, and in particular, the work of their center forward, Hiroaki Nakazawa, gave fits to the Cavaliers. Speedy and relentless, Nakazawa was a 5'4" swarm of gnats that the Cavs just could not shake. Are you familiar with the cartoon character the Tasmanian Devil? Well, if you imagine Taz in fast forward, that's a pretty good representation of Nakazawa. He was relentless in his pursuit of the ball. Whenever he got knocked down by one of the bigger UVA defenders, Nakazawa bounced back up like a rubber ball and continued the chase. He was a blur of perpetual motion and an ever-present specter of danger.

By the middle of the second half, it was clear that the UVA defense was rattled. The defenders looked panicked and clumsy if the ball was at their feet and Nakazawa was in the same zip code. Virginia's defenders had made some narrow escapes and their luck wasn't going to last forever. They wanted no part of losing the ball to a speedy opponent in such a dangerous part of the field, and that's how they began to play: like players who were afraid to lose the ball. It was a shining example of how pressure can unravel even the most talented players.

The crowd of seven thousand, and me among them, became enamored of Nakazawa for all the same reasons movie audiences are enamored of Rocky: Nakazawa's commitment to the cause was unwavering. In spite of the odds, he refused to be deterred. No matter what UVA did to him, no matter how many times they knocked him down, he just kept coming. His relentlessness was downright inspiring!

The match had been promoted as an exhibition. The Cavs weren't looking for the kind of game that Wesleyan brought that day, and they certainly weren't anticipating the headaches brought on by Nakazawa. He was single-handedly making Virginia hate it. He was a constant threat to nick the ball from the UVA defense, and his work rate and determination were big reasons that the crowd swung in Wesleyan's favor. When Nakazawa was chopped down in the UVA goal box, the crowd's conversion was complete. The seven thousand in attendance had clearly morphed into a pro-Wesleyan crowd.

So far I've emphasized organization over work rate, because without organization, the work rate becomes pretty inconsequential. By that same token, if you're going to be a high-pressure team, organization is meaningless if you don't have the players who are willing to bust their tails. High pressure can do great things, but it requires an incredible mental and physical commitment, particularly from your players up front. They have to be willing to chase and tackle and block clearances. They have to take bodily risks and commit to serious physical demands. They are the tip of your spear. They are the ones leading the charge, and unless they lead that charge with courage, passion and fury, the battle will be lost.

It's up to you to decide if high pressure is a good fit for your personnel. When it came to matters of recruiting, my old boss, Steve Holeman, was fond of saying that if you need someone to climb a tree, you can either train a horse or hire a squirrel. I believe that you have to pick a system and a style that fits the players you have available and not the other way around. If you plan to be an all-out high pressure team, you need to have some serious grinders up front, and I don't know if that's a quality everyone has inside of them. Some players grind because it's their nature. Some players can be coached into grinders. And unfortunately, some will never fully commit to the work ethic that high pressure demands. My point is, if you intend to play high pressure, make sure you've got a lot of squirrels. Otherwise you'll never climb that tree.

EXERCISES FOR TEACHING HIGH-PRESSURE

Training High Pressure

I f you've read some of my other books, you'll recognize quite a few of the exercises in this section. Some of them appeared in *Shutout Pizza*, which makes sense because that was a book about defending. Some of the others have appeared in my books as attacking exercises, but we can convert them into defensive-themed drills by simply coaching the other side of the ball. This is by no means an exhaustive collection of exercises for teaching high pressure. My hope is to provide some quality drills that you can immediately incorporate into your training, and to also get you thinking about how you can tweak your own attacking drills to address the topic of high pressure defending.

1v1 Tunnel

The grid is roughly 10x20. The defender starts at one end of the grid with the ball; the attacker starts at the other end. The defender serves the ball into the attacker and moves out to defend. The attacker scores by dribbling out of the defender's end of the grid. The defender gets a point by either dispossessing the attacker or knocking the ball out of the grid.

This is a pretty common 1v1 exercise that focuses on individual attacking and defending. We're going to tweak this drill to make it more applicable to high pressure defending. If we play high pressure, our attackers do a lot of defending, and as we said earlier, we don't want them defending like defenders. We want them to be less patient and more aggressive, so we can make a simple modification to this game to encourage that behavior. All we have to do is mark out a midfield line across the grid. Now the defender only gets a point by winning the ball in the attacker's half of the grid. This encourages the defender to quickly close on the ball and to make a tackle without giving ground.

There are a variety of exercises that can be similarly modified to reward winning the ball in the attacking half of the field.

1v1 Tunnel for High Pressure

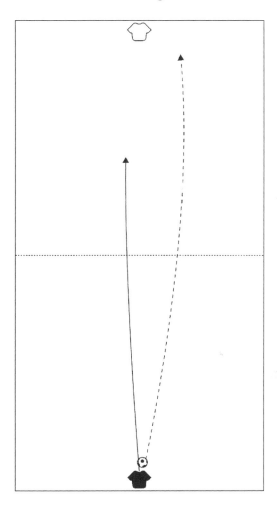

Sheffield
Wednesday

This game is 10v10 on a full field with no goalkeepers. Build a 12-yard arc in front of each goal. No player from either team is allowed in these arcs except to restart play. When a goal is scored, one player from the defending team goes into the goal to retrieve a ball. As soon as he dribbles or passes out of the arc, play is live. There are no corner kicks; if the ball goes over the end-line, possession goes to the defending team and play is restarted as if a goal was scored. Otherwise it's just soccer and offside is in effect (as if there were GKs).

This is one of my all-time favorite games and it serves a lot of purposes, one of which is getting pressure on the ball. The purpose of the arc is to keep the goal unguarded which, in turn, considerably extends shooting range. Basically, all a player needs to do is float a ball over the defense and if it reaches the arc, it'll roll into the goal. From that standpoint, pressure that results in a turnover can be immediately rewarded.

This is a team defending game, and that's really the definition of high pressure. This exercise forces the players to deny turns whenever possible, and to put immediate pressure on the ball when an opponent has turned. It also forces the defending team to quickly adjust and rotate when an opponent has broken pressure. If you're going to be good at high pressure, you need to know what to do when your pressure breaks down.

Sheffield Wednesday

Here is the field design for Sheffield Wednesday.

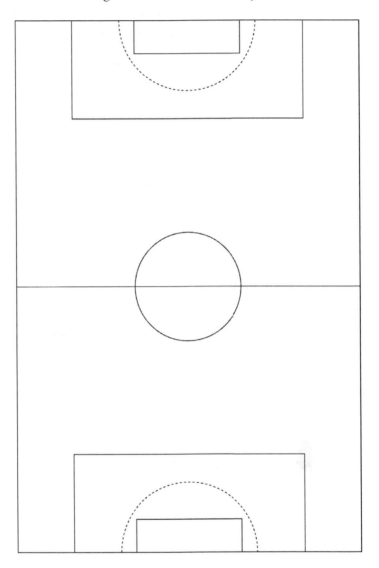

Suicide Kings

Every once in a while I think it's a good idea to just make my players go to war. That's what Suicide Kings is – a war. It's an exercise intended to train the warrior's mentality.

Divide your group into three teams of five for a round robin. It will help if you can create some type of competitive incentive before this exercise commences. You want maximum effort and intensity right from the start.

Each game will last four minutes. Set up a field roughly 40 yards wide by 45 yards long (adjust as necessary). Quite simply, Suicide Kings is a game of 5v5 to full-sided goals with no goalkeepers. The coach stands on the sideline at midfield with a large supply of balls. The game starts with the coach soft-punting a ball onto the field so players can duel for a header. At that point the game is live. Every time the ball leaves the field of play, either over the boundaries or into the goal, the coach immediately soft-punts a new ball onto the field. The team with more goals at the end of four minutes wins. Winners keep the field.

The reason the games are only four minutes long is because this game should be played at a frantic pace. Encourage players to shoot whenever they get the chance. The entire field is within shooting range to an unguarded goal, so defensive pressure must be immediate.

This is a game where work rate, courage and a commitment to winning are rewarded. Players have to be willing to sprint to get pressure on the ball, and they absolutely must be willing to block shots. There's a premium on winning (or at least not losing) individual battles in this exercise, because a lost battle usually ends up with the ball in the back of the net.

I wouldn't rank this highly as a tactical exercise for team defending. Like I mentioned, this is a game about mentality. However, it's not entirely without tactical merit. From a tactical perspective, the most notable benefit is the defensive rotation of players if the player pressuring the ball gets beaten.

This game should be played at a sprint. If your players aren't winded after four minutes, you're doing something wrong. Suicide Kings is sort of a cross between soccer and roller derby, so I wouldn't use it within three days of an actual match because some players are going to get dinged up.

Goalkeeper Targets

This game is 8v8 plus goalkeepers. Play the full width of the field, but shorten the field to seventy yards (that will run one of your end-lines through the top of the center circle). You may also want to shorten the goalkeeper's box to ten or twelve yards for older players. In this game, teams try to target the 'opposing' goalkeeper. In other words, you don't get points for putting the ball in the net; you score by flighting a ball into the opposing goalkeeper, who must catch it out of the air.

This game is philosophically similar to Sheffield Wednesday because if you don't quickly pressure the player on the ball, it's very likely that player will be able to serve into the 'keeper. The difference is that in this game, because the field is so short, a lot of scoring is done from defenders. In Sheffield Wednesday, forwards are often rewarded by dispossessing a defender. In Targets, forwards are punished for not putting defenders under immediate pressure.

This is a super high-paced game that gets players in the habit of working hard to get pressure on the ball.

Dutch Modified

The Dutch game involves three teams. It is a possession game with two of the teams playing keep-away from the third. Let's say the red and blue teams are playing keep-away from yellow. If red gives the ball away to yellow, blue and yellow are immediately playing keep-away from red. When introducing this game, I would start with three players per team on a field that is 35 x 20. This is a big space and will need to be pared down as your players get the hang of it. You can also play this game with four players per team.

This is a fun game once the players start to figure it out. The quick changes in the roles of the teams (attacking or defending) forces the players to stay alert. Often times the ball will be turned over several times in succession, so the players have to figure out which team is the one defending.

Dutch is primarily used as a possession game, but there are a couple of ways we can tweak this game to make it more conducive to teaching high pressure and, more specifically, the idea of pressing the ball immediately after possession has been lost. Both games require that we put the defending team in for a predetermined amount of time, as opposed to having them relinquish the role upon a change of possession.

In the first exercise, we're going to play a round-robin format. We'll make the yellow team the defending unit for the first ninety seconds. The red and blue teams play keep-away from yellow. When yellow wins the ball in-bounds, they get a point for each pass they complete before being dispossessed by their opponents. If yellow has the ball and it gets knocked out of bounds, the ball is restarted with the red/blue teams. At the end of ninety seconds, the yellows switch roles with one of the other teams until all three teams have had a turn. At the end of three rounds, the team with the highest score wins.

In this game, the defending team is the only team to score. The attacking teams prevent that by either keeping the ball, or by winning it back quickly once possession has been lost. Even as they are possessing the ball, the attackers have to be prepared to react immediately to a turnover.

The Dutch Game

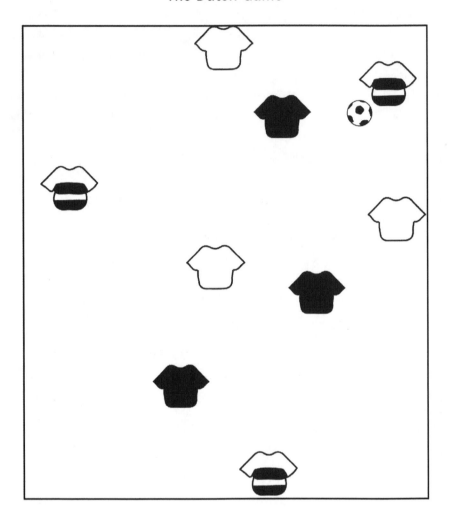

Dutch with Counters

We're going to use the exact same format as we did in Dutch Modified, with three teams playing a round-robin format and with each team serving as the defensive group for a predetermined period of time. The defending team is again the only team that can score. The difference is that now we are going to set up some goals around the outside of the playing grid. Now, when the defending team takes possession, they have goals to shoot at. This put the onus on the attacking teams to quickly shift gears once possession has been lost.

You can use mini-goals, actual goals with goalkeepers, or a combination of the two. I recommend using four goals, one for each side of your grid. Set the goals ten yards back from the grid boundary. Just one note, the players can't leave the grid. In other words, if a player on the defending team wins the ball, he can't dribble out of the grid and then shoot.

In both of these Dutch games, a focus on possession is balanced out by the need to press immediately once the ball has been turned over, and that's often the ingredient that coaches don't stress enough in their possession exercises. Coaches tend to want possession exercises that are smooth and pretty. When you start incentivizing the defenders, the drill can turn downright ugly, but that's a problem you've got to embrace because it's what you'll see on game day,

It doesn't matter how many possession exercises you do; during the course of a game, you're going to lose the ball. How your players respond to those moments will have a major impact on your success.

Dutch with Counters

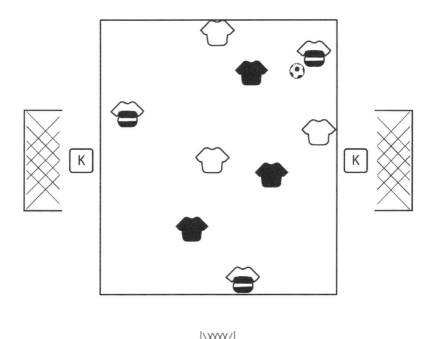

6-3-1 Rush

This is another possession game that we're going to use to teach pressure. As a possession game, the focus is on the attacking side being able to keep the ball in a tight space under heavy pressure. As a pressure game, we're just going to coach the defending team into chasing like dogs. Yes, we can talk about things like angles of approach and angles of the supporting defenders, but this game moves incredibly fast so it's not super-conducive to making coaching points. From the standpoint of defending, it's just about hard freaking work and a relentless commitment to dispossessing the opponent.

Make a grid that's 15x15 or smaller. Divide into two teams of seven players. The red team starts in the grid and will be the attacking team for 90 seconds. Designate one of the attackers as the central player (indicated by the striped jersey). The blue team starts at one corner, outside of the grid. All of the balls start with the coach. The game begins when the coach knocks a ball into a red player. At that moment, three blues come rushing into the grid to defend. Their objective is to knock the ball out of the grid as fast as possible. Every time the red team strings together five consecutive passes, it scores a point. (Another way to score this exercise is to award the attacking team a point for every pass it connects in to the central player.)

Every time the ball leaves the grid, the blue team replaces its three players with three new ones and a new ball is immediately served in to the red team. To be clear, as soon as one ball leaves the grid, the next ball is served into the grid. This is a physically demanding game and requires a lot of hard work from the defending team, which is something you're going to need if you intend to play high-pressure soccer.

6-3-1 Rush

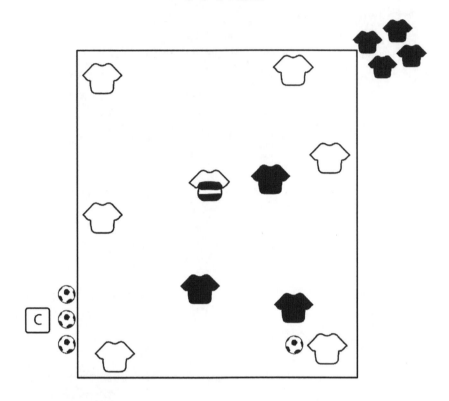

Cross the River

H ere is yet another possession exercise that we can utilize as a pressing drill by changing our focus to the team without the ball, or, more specifically, the team that has just lost the ball.

Make a grid that is roughly 30x15, then divide it into three smaller grids of 10x15. Have a server with plenty of soccer balls stationed just wide of the middle grid. Divide into two teams of five. In one of the end grids, start with five reds playing keep-away from two blues. The middle grid is empty. The final grid has the remaining three blue players. (You can also play this game at 6v6, with a 6v3 situation in the grid with the ball. Just make the end grids bigger.)

The attacking team scores by stringing together five consecutive passes. There is no limit to the amount of points they can score on any given turn. If they connect 20 consecutive passes before losing the ball, they score four points. The defending team's objective is to knock the ball out of the grid as quickly as possible. As soon as the ball leaves the grid, the coach sends a new ball down to the grid with the three blues. Their teammates race back to that grid to support them, as do two red players who will serve as defenders. That leaves three reds waiting in the initial grid. Now the blues are trying to score points. When the ball leaves the blues' grid, the coach serves the next ball into the grid with the three reds, and the game plays on like that.

The optimal time to score points in this game is immediately upon a change of possession, before the defending team has arrived to defend. Therefore, the ability of the defending/pressing team to quickly move into the opposing grid will often impact the success of the attacking team. The sooner the pressers move in to defend, the better off their team will be.

This game demands a lot of hard work on the defensive end, and that's a good habit for a pressing team. However, there's another valuable concept that you can squeeze out of this drill, and that's eliminating the pause. As a member of the attacking team, at any given moment you might be transitioned into a member of the defending unit. Recognizing that the ball is going to be lost, and making that transition, will give you a head start on your pressing journey, and that's another habit we want our players to develop. The sooner we recognize the time to press, the more successful our press will be.

Cross the River

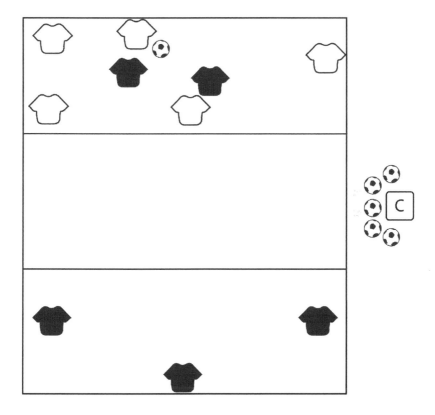

101

1 01 is my all-time favorite possession game. It's played between the eighteen
and midfield, and sideline to sideline. It's a good idea to have a scorekeeper
assigned to each team, because there's a lot of fast math in this one.

Quite simply, it's 9v9 plus a neutral player playing keep-away. Balls that
go out of bounds can be restarted with kick-ins, throw-ins, or a combination
of the two – that's for you to decide. This is strictly a possession game. There
are no goals to attack. There are no touch restrictions, but teams only score a
point each time they successfully connect a one-touch pass. The first team to
101 wins.

Once your team begins to develop a mastery of this exercise, you can spice
up the scoring system with options like these: A team is awarded five points for
a successful wall pass around an opponent. A team receives a five-point bonus
for a flighted pass over 25 yards that concludes with a successful one-touch
layoff. A team will lose five points if it gives away the restart after the ball has
gone out of bounds.

Okay, that's the attacking side of this exercise. I have to confess that until the attacking element of this game reaches a certain level of proficiency, you should probably hold off on addressing the pressing aspect. In other words, if the teams can't string five consecutive passes with some degree of regularity, it's just going to be chaos.

However, if at least one of the teams can keep the ball for an extended period of time, the result will be two teams in different shapes. The team that can hold the ball will be more spread out, while the opponent will condense its shape in an effort to win possession. This is what best sets up the counter-press, both tactically and psychologically.

When the team in possession loses the ball, chances are they've lost it to the tightly packed gaggle of opponents. This is where maximum effort and urgency should be applied to win the ball back before the opponent has formed an attacking shape and can escape pressure.

As much as I love this game for its possession element, I am equally fond of the opportunities it presents to address counter-pressing. It's all fine and dandy when you're stringing your seventeenth consecutive pass, but how do you react when the ball is turned over? Teaching that moment where recognition turns into action is the critical component to counter-pressing.

Possession in Systems

P ossession in Systems is played between the eighteens using the full width of the field and ten players on each team. Each team sets up in a system such as a 4-4-2 or 4-2-3-1. There are no goalkeepers. The offside rule is in effect. There are various ways to score this depending on what your objectives are.

My favorite scoring system for this drill is to award a point for every one-touch pass a team connects in its attacking half of the field. The pass must originate and be received in the attacking half. I like this variation because it encourages players to keep the ball *and* advance it up the park. Some teams can keep the ball for eons if they go sideways or backwards, but they really struggle to go forward. This gives your team the confidence to keep the ball in the opponent's end of the field.

I also like this scoring system for the incentive it creates to win back the ball in the opponent's end of the field. When we first implemented this exercise on a regular basis, our focus was on the element of possession, but we quickly realized the value of emphasizing immediate pressure once possession was lost. In this exercise, there's a tremendous incentive to keep the opponent from reaching your end of the field, so it naturally aligns itself with the ideals of a high-pressure system. This is an excellent drill for coaching the six-second rule.

If you use this game, I would suggest focusing on the possession end of things until your team gets comfortable keeping the ball in the opponent's half. Once the players have a decent handle on that, then introduce the pressuring aspect.

This became one of my favorite exercises for teaching high pressure because it is very game-like and the players must learn to recognize and react quickly to the cues. It can help eliminate that pause between losing the ball and realizing that you now need to put pressure on it.

Team Press

This is a simple 11v11 set-up. All field players start in the middle third, so the lines of defenders are a solid forty-five yards out in front of their own goals. The coach starts somewhere near midfield with the ball, then dumps it into an awkward position behind the back four. The idea is to put a defender in a position where she is first to the ball but with pressure on her back. The objective for her team is to play its way out of the pressure and attack the opponent's goal. The objective for the pressing team is to force a turnover and attack the goal.

This is a very choppy exercise, especially if the outside backs don't mind hoofing the ball over the sideline. As the coach, it's critical that you don't waste repetitions by hitting your serves into an area where the goalkeeper will be first to the ball. Goalkeepers will cheat like crazy during this exercise, so if you catch yours being a little too positionally ambitious, don't be shy about lobbing one over her head every now and then just to keep her honest.

The coaching objective for this exercise is to organize your pressure. I would recommend stopping play as soon as you see any type of positional errors. You can correct those errors and restart play where you left off, or you may have to just restart with a new repetition.

This isn't an exercise I would spend much more than fifteen minutes on at any one time. It's physically demanding and is prone to reps that end with a ball out of bounds. But there is gold to be found in the good reps, so I wouldn't ignore it either. We typically would use this exercise for ten to fifteen minutes and then just step out of the way and let it morph into a full-field scrimmage.

11v11 Squeeze

I mentioned this exercise in the *Staying Connected* chapter, but I also wanted to include it in this section to make your life a little easier should you want to reference the drills.

This is simply an 11v11 exercise with one restriction: Every field player must reach midfield before his team can score. If the ball crosses the goal-line and a player from the attacking team hasn't reached midfield, the goal does not count.

This forces both teams into a high-pressure style, which opens up the space behind the defenders and leads to quick counterattacks. Those counterattacks force the second and third layers to sprint up the field, and that in turn keeps all the layers connected.

The real benefit of this game isn't when those quick counterattacks lead to a goal, but rather when those counterattacks break down and the opponent takes possession deep in its own territory. Now the team that launched the counter has its layers connected in the opponent's half and is positioned to press up high. This is an excellent game for keeping your layers connected and moving forward as a unit.

Lateral Compactness

A lot of players think in terms of *position* instead of *positioning*. It can be downright alien for a left-midfielder to pinch centrally, or for a right wing to slide all the way to the opposing right center back, but when we press, we need to crowd the ball-side of the field, and these are adjustments that must be made. This exercise is simply 11v11 on a full field that has been divided into four zones that run from end-line to end-line. The idea is that when the opponent has the ball in one of the two widest zones, our team squeezes to that side of the field and vacates the two weak-side zones. The zones are set up to be instructional landmarks as opposed to restrictions on the game. In other words, there's no insta-penalty for failing to be in a proper zone (unless you want to create a penalty). You can also create variations of this game using three or five zones. You can also fold these zones into other exercises like the 11v11 Squeeze game.

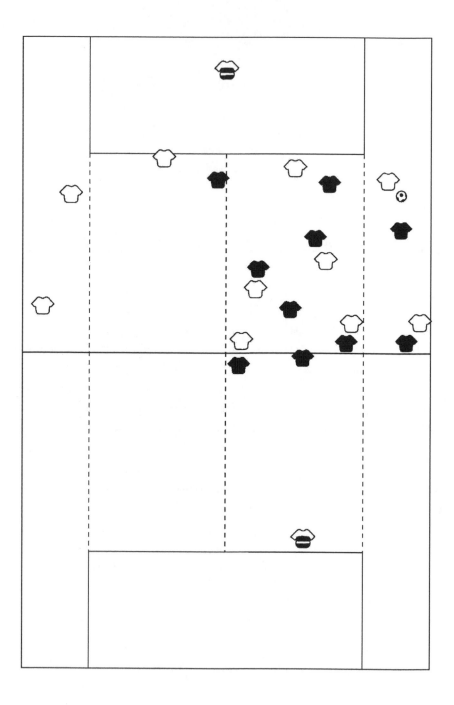

Three-Goal Game

H ere's a game your goalkeeper will hate, which is reason enough to give it a whirl. It's a great exercise if you want to work on switching fields, but if we flip it around and focus on the other team, it's also an excellent game for teaching lateral compaction in high pressure. Play 11v11 using the full width of the field but only 80 yards of the length. On one end-line there is a centrally located goal. On the other end-line, position two goals, each one about ten yards in from the sideline. The 'pressing' team is defending the end with two goals, but they only have one goalkeeper. That 'keeper is responsible for guarding both goals. Start the game by knocking a ball into a defender on the 'non-pressing' team. The ultimate objective for the non-pressing team is to break pressure and attack the unguarded goal. It is critical that the pressing team keep the opponent from switching fields. If the opponent executes a big switch, the pressing team must immediately adjust to prevent the opponent from shooting at the unguarded goal.

There is offside, but the offside line remains at midfield, so there are only twenty yards of offside territory on one end of the field. If you want to reward the pressing team more liberally, you can set up the lone goal as you would in Sheffield Wednesday.

Three-Goal Game

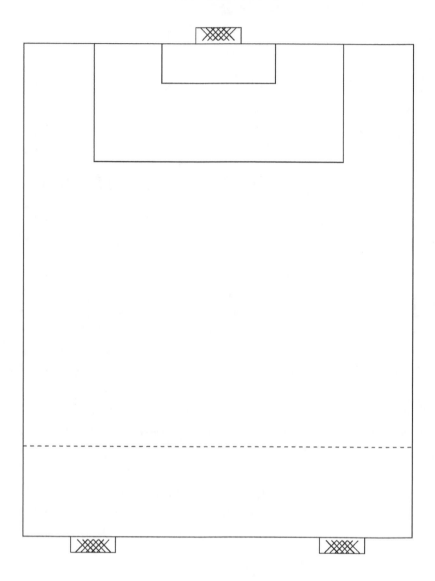

STOPPAGE TIME

The Hornet's Nest

It was a Saturday morning in Oxford, MS. Steve Holeman and I were watching the video of our match from the previous night. It was a night when our high pressure had given fits to a very good opponent and we were bathing in the afterglow of a hard-won victory. We watched as our players chased down opponents, hawking the ball from one space to the next, forcing turnover after turnover in rapid succession. The video had only been playing for five minutes when Steve commented, "It looks like someone kicked over a hornet's nest." It couldn't have been said any better. It was a master class of organized bedlam and it had clearly rattled our opponent into a state of emotional disarray. I had remarked during the game that our opponents were going to need counseling at half-time.

I'm a fan of high pressure because it lets my team play the game on our terms – or at least on my terms. It's fast-paced and physical. It rewards aggression and work rate and forces the opponent to produce an answer. In other words, it forces the other team to be splendid at technical execution. And if they can't do it, they're in trouble. But there's another element of high pressure that I love – an element that coaching books don't mention – and that's the camaraderie it builds. When you play pretty much all-out high pressure, there's a level of work rate, selflessness and courage that has to be factored into the recipe. If you're lacking those qualities, high pressure won't produce for you. But when a team full of players buys into the philosophy of high pressure and selflessly executes that philosophy on game day, they are driven together by a commitment to their teammates and a commitment to the mission. There is nothing in soccer so satisfying as walking off the field knowing that your pressure made the opponent hate it.

High pressure soccer doesn't just require the right athletes; it requires the *right people* – hard working, courageous people who can set aside their individual egos for the sake of the mission. It requires players who are willing to grind just so a teammate may be the beneficiary of their work. High pressure requires selflessness because every player is so dependent on her teammates. If you're going to teach high pressure, you have to preach selflessness. You have to get your players to drop their personal agendas (and possibly the agendas of their parents). Make no mistake about it, high pressure is a *team* project.

High pressure isn't just about athletes or tactics. You can check those boxes and still lack the chemistry to effectively execute. For high pressure to consistently deliver, your players have to be more than players – they have to first be teammates. You need players who genuinely value the higher calling of teamwork. You need a team full of people willing to dig ditches and take the physical risks for the greater good. It's just that simple. It isn't easy, but when you get that right group of people together on the field at the same time, all of them committing to aggressively press the opponent, it can be a most beautiful thing. And when those players walk off the field after a match, they are bonded more closely than when they walked onto it, because they know that they've given everything to their teammates, and that their teammates have given everything in return. And that is about the best thing you can get from a sport.

A FINAL WORD

Thanks for reading my book! I hope you enjoyed it and feel that you got your money's worth. There are as many different coaching philosophies as there are coaches. Plenty of coaches will disagree with some of the material in this book and that's fine. If every coach subscribed to the same philosophy, soccer would be a pretty boring game. I just wanted to present my views on high pressure defending and provide some exercises to help you teach it. I'm not saying this is the only way, just that it's my way. My advice is to take the parts that made sense to you and incorporate them into your team. Then just leave the rest behind.

If you enjoyed this book, I would be most grateful if you would take a moment of your time to leave me a review on Amazon. It will only take you a minute, but those five-star reviews are the most valuable tip you can put in an author's jar.

If you'd like to purchase copies of this book for everyone on your team at a discounted rate, just contact me through the soccerpoet.com website.

I invite you to read my blog at www.soccerpoet.com. And I hope you'll be my Twitter friend. My handle is @SoccerPoet.

If you'd like to hire me to run a camp for your team or to speak at an event, contact me through the soccerpot.com website.

I'd like to thank Gavin Donaldson, the head coach at West Virginia Wesleyan, for graciously taking a stroll with me down memory lane. Thanks to Phil Jones, Danny McNally and Dom Martelli for their insights. Thanks to

Aaron Usiskin for the diagrams, and thanks to Rob Marino, Jack Shafer, Kate Burkholder and Paul Denfeld for their proofreading and editing expertise.

Thank you to my daughter and best friend, Izzy – I hope I made you proud. I love you and I miss you every day.

OTHER BOOKS BY DAN BLANK

Soccer iQ Volume 1 – The #1 international best-seller and an NSCAA Soccer Journal Top 5 Book of the Year. Named the #1 Book for Players and Coaches by Football.com. The only how-to book written specifically for soccer players. Watch the companion videos on the SoccerPoet YouTube channel. Download the free companion quiz at www.soccerpoet.com.

Soccer iQ Volume 2 – More simple and effective strategies for becoming a smarter soccer player. (All the great stuff I forgot to include in Volume 1!)

Everything Your Coach Never Told You Because You're a Girl – This is what your coaches would have said to you if you were a boy, told through the story of a small-college team that won more games than it ever had a right to win. It's a straightforward look at the qualities that define the most competitive females.

HAPPY FEET – How to Be a Gold Star Soccer Parent (Everything the Coach, the Ref and Your Kid Want You to Know) – The book that coaches want parents to read! If you want to maintain your sanity as a coach, *HAPPY FEET* is the best gift you can give a soccer parent! This book includes free companion videos to explain some of soccer's more mysterious concepts such as the advantage rule, offside, soccer systems and combination play. It also explains the most common errors that well-meaning soccer parents make without even realizing it. Prevent headaches before they start by getting soccer parents to read this book.

ROOKIE – Surviving Your Freshman Year of College Soccer – The ultimate survival guide for the rising college freshman. If your players are planning to play at the college level, give them a head start. I can't possibly explain how much easier their lives will be if they just read this book.

POSSESSION — Teaching Your Team to Keep the Darn Ball — A book for coaches of all levels who want their teams to pass the ball and pass it well. It combines a thorough explanation of possession concepts with 30 practical possession exercises to help your team develop its ability to keep the ball. Easy-to-understand diagrams help you visualize the layout and design of these exercises. More importantly, the exercises include explanations about the critical coaching points *and* the most common mistakes the players will make when playing these exercises.

Shutout Pizza — Smarter Soccer Defending for Players and Coaches — Ole Miss led the SEC in goals-against average in 2009. Georgia did it in 2010. This is the book those players used to become the league's best defense.

ABOUT THE AUTHOR

Dan Blank has been coaching college soccer for over twenty years. He is the only coach in Southeastern Conference history to lead the conference's best defense in consecutive years at different universities (Ole Miss 2009, Georgia 2010). He has an 'A' License from the USSF and an Advanced National Diploma from the NSCAA. He has written eight books including the international best-seller, *Soccer iQ*. You can buy his books and read his blog at www.soccerpoet.com.

Made in the
USA
Monee, IL